The Sounds and Spelling Patterns of English

Phonics for Teachers and Parents

Phyllis E. Fischer

University of Maine at Farmington

Oxton House, Publishers
Morrill, Maine

Send orders and correspondence to: Oxton House, Publishers
P. O. Box 25
Morrill, ME 04952-0025

LB
1573.3
F57
1993

Printed in the United States of America
using soya ink on recycled paper.

10 9 8 7 6 5 4 3 2

ISBN 1-881929-01-9

To Bill

Preface

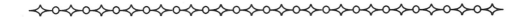

This book has been written in response to questions from practicing teachers, from parents, and—most often—from students in my college courses, many of whom have been practicing teachers and parents. They have asked,

> Which word families should the students in my class be able to read by now?

> What skills does Sara need to learn in order to read this book?

> I am home-schooling my children; what reading skills should I teach them?

> Why do we spell *happening* with one *n* before the *ing*, but *beginning* with two *n*'s?

and many, many other questions of this sort. In response, I used to write short handouts for my students, so that they would not have to rely on quickly written notes when they wanted to refer to the answer. As I gave a stack of these handouts to a teacher or a parent, I was often asked why I don't just write a book that explains the sounds and spelling patterns that we need in order to read and write English. So I did.

The most basic sounds and spelling patterns are sometimes included in textbooks on teaching reading, but this discussion usually is brief when it does exist and, with the present emphasis on literature-based reading instruction, it is appearing less and less. A description of phonics, as the sounds and spelling patterns are often called collectively, is also imbedded in books and other materials used for teaching phonics. In these materials, however, the patterns are described only as they are needed for teaching a particular sound or spelling pattern being introduced in the material. Missing from the current literature is an overview of the structure of our written words that provides readers with an understanding of how the sounds of English are paired with the spelling patterns. This book presents that overview.

Most of us, as proficient readers and spellers of English, learned the sounds and their spelling patterns quite some time ago, and we use them daily without paying conscious attention to them. Therefore, few of us are cognizant of the patterns, and even fewer of us can describe them to someone else without some explicit learning or review on our part. Many children learn to read words with little direct instruction from their primary grade teachers; those children have strong natural abilities relevant to that task and they often have a lot of indirect and direct assistance from parents, Sesame Street, and other people who read to them and play many of the sound games that develop reading skills. Many other children, however, learn to read words only poorly, if at all, unless their teachers teach them explicitly about the sounds and spelling patterns. Some of these children come to school without the years of literacy instruction other children have had, and some of them have a learning disability that makes it very difficult to learn to read words. Sadly, all too many people do not receive the instruction they need in order to learn these skills, even by the time they leave our high schools, often because their teachers are unable to transform their own intuitive understanding of the structures of English into explicit concepts that they can communicate to their students.

The Sounds and Spelling Patterns of English is written for anyone who is or will be involved, directly or indirectly, in teaching someone to read words. Since it delineates the scope of the task of decoding English words, it can be used as a primary text in courses that focus on various methods for teaching reading-decoding and spelling, or as a supplementary text in virtually any course about reading skills. It supplies the content of an important piece of the reading task, thereby providing the conceptual background necessary for informed discussions about how best to help students learn the phonics skills. Although it is not a manual on how to teach this material, it includes some tips on teaching these sounds and patterns, especially tips on *when* it makes most sense to teach some of them. It is, thereby, a useful book for teachers whose students are becoming proficient at reading words but need help with some of the patterns, and also for people who are skillful at using a variety of teaching techniques with new content and at preparing their own materials to teach that content. Moreover, since this book provides specific descriptions of the sounds and spelling patterns that must be mastered if someone is to become a proficient reader, it can be helpful to people involved in someone's reading instruction through informal conferences with educators, or through a formal Individualized Educational Plan (IEP).

For courses devoted to teaching and learning phonics skills, this book provides a concise, but fairly detailed, description of the scope of the task, as well as some comments about sequence possibilities. Since it explains the content piece of an extremely important part of the reading task, it is particularly useful as a basis for class discussions about the intersection of content, student characteristics, and teaching models. The teaching tips in the book imply, for the most part, a direct-instruction teaching model for this material. That certainly is not the only model that makes sense and, indeed, may not be the most interesting treatment of it with some students. However, having used different models of instruction with students of varying ages and readiness skills, and having examined the research related to the characteristics and learning of students who are at risk for failure in reading, I have concluded that the content of reading-decoding is best taught by direct instruction to at least three groups of students:

— Students who are beginning the formal schooling process without strong backgrounds in literacy tasks. The speed with which these decoding skills can be acquired with direct instruction leaves time for such crucial tasks as writing, sharing writing and books with peers and teachers, or thinking and talking about reasons for wanting to read and write.

— Older students who have not succeeded in learning to read words. Direct instruction improves skills quickly, allowing the students to see and measure their own successes, and to gain confidence rapidly as more and more skills are added to their decoding repertoire.

— Students who are learning English as a second language. All of the same reasons apply to these students. The direct-instruction teaching tips in this book have been used very successfully with educationally disadvantaged children of all ages from homes and neighborhoods where English is not often spoken.

Appendix A lists all the regularly-used sounds for the letter units that spell English words. It provides a concise reference source for reviewing the sounds and spelling patterns you already know and examining patterns that you may not have noticed before. This reference list should be particularly helpful if you intend to teach these sounds and spelling patterns. Appendix B lists most of the prefixes and suffixes encountered in nontechnical English, with their common meanings and examples of their use, as a reference for teachers who are working with multisyllabic words. The worksheets and exercises are intended to provide the practice for mastery of the concepts introduced. If you are using this book to understand the overall structure of English words, but will not be teaching the sounds or spelling patterns, you might want to complete just enough of the worksheets and exercises to understand the concepts without memorizing the specific examples, and you might want to peruse Appendix A for comments on structure without focusing on the sounds of the individual letters. If you are teaching reading-decoding skills to beginning readers, the worksheets can also be used directly with your students.

⬖⬖⬖ Acknowledgments ⬖⬖⬖

I am delighted to begin my acknowledgements by thanking all of the children who have inspired me to learn more so that I could help them be better at reading and thinking. I especially want to mention the third-grade children of Hopkins, Minnesota, who, during my first two years of teaching, showed me how fascinating the learning process can be—and what meagre knowledge I had about the intersection of individual learning characteristics and the content of the task at hand. Of the many students I have worked with since my graduate school professors helped me fill the most glaring of those gaps, I especially want to thank the third graders at the Truman School in New Haven, Connecticut, and Greg Edwards, who challenged me to describe the sounds and spelling patterns of English in ways that are clear and interesting to young children and to children for whom the patterns are not readily obvious. Of the many mentors and colleagues who have been instrumental in focusing my energies on the process of reading-decoding, special thanks go to Betty Gallistel, Isabelle Liberman, Dani Zinna, Lucy Duffy, and Beth Taylor for intellectual stimulation and enjoyment. Though it is impossible to mention individually the many university students who have challenged, stimulated, and reinforced my efforts, the students of all ages who have shown me unique ways of learning and allowed me to test my theories and teaching methods, and all the parents who have helped me understand the frustrations and dreams that keep them searching for people who can help their children learn to read, my heartfelt gratitude extends to each and every one.

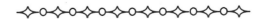

Contents

I

A Few Words about Words

⟨▧▧▧▧▧▧▧▧▧▧▧▧▧▧▧▧▧▧▧▧▧▧▧▧▧▧▧▧▧▧▧▧▧▧▧▧▧⟩

> **phonics** [*noun; plural form, but takes singular verb*] (1) the study of sound; (2) the method of using the sounds of a language when teaching people to read; or (3) (more recently) the letter–sound correspondences themselves.
>
> **ortho-** [*prefix; from the Greek orthos, straight*] correct, proper, or standard.
>
> **-graph** [*suffix; from the Greek graphein, to write*] indicates something that writes, draws, or records; something that is written, drawn, or recorded in some way. [*telegraph, photograph*]
>
> **orthography** [*noun*] the study or systematic use of standard, proper, or correct spelling of the words in a language. (The study of orthography means the study of the standard, proper, or correct sequences of letters in a written language system.)
>
> **code** [*noun*] a system of symbols or signals used to transmit messages.

The teaching of phonics, or of English orthography, is the teaching of a code. The letters of our alphabet are the symbols of the code, and the spelling patterns tell us which sounds to use when decoding words. While well-known to those of us who are proficient readers, this code is not well-known to beginning readers. Many beginning readers figure out the code of their native language with little apparent difficulty; many others have trouble deciphering that code. Although parents and Sesame Street provide a great

1

deal of informal teaching of the code, teachers are primarily responsible for teaching the orthographic structure of our language. Regardless of the particular teaching method used, beginning readers somehow must come to understand this structure. In order to teach the code to would-be readers who are having difficulty, it is essential that we ourselves know its structure explicitly. As proficient readers, we have mastered using the code, but most of us did not learn the components and rules of the code overtly. We cannot teach the code to others until we learn these components and rules. The purpose of this book is to present and explain labels for the components of the code—to demystify the orthographic structure of English.

Since English does not have a one-to-one correspondence between sounds and letters (e.g., *c* is pronounced both /k/ as in *cat* and /s/ as in *city*), effective teaching of the code requires that we teach both the usual sounds of letters or letter groups and the spelling patterns (the orthographic structure) of the language. Both of these are required for a reader to know when to use a particular sound for a letter unit when reading and when to use a particular letter unit for a sound when spelling. When we use direct instruction to teach this code, we often say that we are "teaching phonics." However, the word "phonics" is used to mean a variety of things in education: Some people use it to describe just the sounds of the letters; others use it to describe the letter sounds and the orthographic structure; still others use it to describe a process of analyzing the sound patterns of words the reader *can already* read. In this book, "phonics" is used as a concise label for the entire code, including both the sounds and the orthographic structure.

A few notes are in order before beginning the actual work of the book. First, there are many fine gradations of sounds that occur in the ordinary speech of individuals (see the definition of "phoneme," below). For example, the sound of the *a* in *man* is slightly different than the sound of the *A* in *Agatha* for many speakers of English, even though both *a*'s have the short vowel sound. These slight differences usually are not important when you are teaching phonics. Beginning readers are almost always able to make sound shifts such as these with no apparent difficulty. This is also true when you are teaching readers whose regional dialects are different than yours. You may teach them the sound for a letter as you use it, but when putting the sound into words, readers will almost always adapt it quite easily to their own dialects. It is the teacher's responsibility to listen to the learners' pronunciation patterns and adjust the lessons as necessary to accommodate the learners. For example, if you pronounce "roof" as /ro͞of/ but the beginning readers you are teaching pronounce it /ro͝of/, you should put it with the other words that use /o͝o/ for *oo*.

As you might have inferred from the previous sentence, the convention used to display a sound in print is to put the letter or letter group that most commonly represents that sound between slashes. Thus, the sound for *m* is written as /m/ and is read as "mmm." The sound for *ph* is written as /f/, and the sound for *c* is written as /k/ when *c* has the so-called "hard" sound and as /s/ when *c* has the "soft" sound. The symbol /c/ is never used to represent a sound because we have both the /k/ and the /s/ to indicate the two different sounds for this letter. The sounds for *g* are written as /g/ [as in *goat*] and /j/ [as in *gem*]; since there is no other letter for /g/, the sound notation and the written symbol use the same letter. A listing of the correspondences between the letter symbols (the "graphemes") and their sounds (the "phonemes") appears in Appendix A.

In this book, italic print is used to indicate a letter or a word considered as a pattern to decode (to pronounce), not as a unit of meaning. Thus, when you read *man*, focus on the sound pattern of *m*, *a*, and *n*, not on the meaning of the word. When you read *Agatha*, focus on *Ag*, *a*, and *tha*, not on a possible person. When the meaning of a word is the focus of attention, single quotation marks are used. Thus, for 'moose', focus on the largest animal of the deer family, native to the northern U.S. and Canada, but for *moose*, focus on *m*, *oo*, and *se*.

The labels used for orthographic structures are generally the same as those commonly used by other educators. Occasionally, however, an alternate label has been chosen because it provides a pedagogically better way of grouping letter combinations than the usual label does. Each of these alternate labels is identified and the rationale for choosing it over the traditional label is described when it is introduced.

Most of us learned some spelling "rules," such as "*i* before *e* except after *c* or when sounded like *a*, as in *neighbor* or *weigh*." While many of these rules apply most of the time, almost all of them have exceptions; indeed, some of the rules have more exceptions than instances. An example of this is the often-taught rule that when two vowels go together the first one does the talking and the second does the walking, or, the first one says its name and the second one is silent. Common instances are *rain*, *seed*, and *boat*. However, the exceptions—as exemplified by *maul*, *boil*, *steak*, *room*, *eight*, and *height*—account for 55% of the cases! For this reason, several professionals in the field of reading are encouraging us to use the word "generalization" to refer to the symbol ⇔ sound patterns that we might previously have called rules—and to be more careful about what we teach. In keeping with that advice, this book refers to the symbol ⇔ sound patterns as either "generalizations" or "patterns," rather than as "rules."

The formal language needed for a precise and efficient discussion of the sound/symbol distinctions begins with the following two definitions.

phoneme [*noun*] any one of the smallest, most basic units of sound in a spoken language.

grapheme [*noun*] a letter or grouping of letters that represents a single phoneme.

Because a grapheme can have any number of letters, it is more precise to talk about a grapheme ⇔ phoneme correspondence than a letter ⇔ sound correspondence. For example, *t*, *sh*, *tch*, *dge*, and *ay* are all graphemes in that they each represent a phoneme (/t/, /sh/, /ch/, /j/, and /ā/); *c*, *k*, *ck*, *ch*, and *que* are all graphemes for the phoneme /k/ (as in *cat*, *kite*, *sock*, *Chris*, and *antique*, respectively). For convenience, we shall often abbreviate the phrase "represents the phoneme(s)" by the symbol ⇒. Thus, the statement

the grapheme *ay* represents the phoneme /ā/

can be written

$$ay \Rightarrow /ā/$$

and can be read informally as

"*ay* has the sound /ā/"   or   "*ay* says /ā/."

Because there are many graphemes for several of the phonemes, and because there are usually no generalizations that tell you which grapheme to use for a phoneme, spelling is difficult for many people. For example, there are eight ways of spelling /ā/, with a generalization for only *ay* and *ey*. Moreover, the generalization only tells you that *ay* and *ey* are not usually used in the middle of syllables; it does *not* say when to use *ay* and when to use *ey*.

diacritical [*adjective*] distinguishing.

diacritical mark a mark or sign affixed to a letter to specify the sound it represents in a particular situation.

Dictionaries use diacritical marks to indicate which sound to give to a letter unit (i.e., which phoneme to give to a grapheme). In teaching reading, we usually do not teach the marks for the varying consonant sounds, probably because there are so few that cannot be represented by a standard letter and because, prior to computers, it took a special typewriter to print the symbols for sounds such as the voiced and unvoiced *th*. We do, however, teach the marks for vowel sounds.

The conventions for diacritical marks used in dictionaries change over time. During the past twenty-five years, there has been a major move toward simplification. For example, most American dictionaries used to indicate the short vowel sound with the ˘ mark, but now some of them indicate the short vowel sounds by using just the letter for the vowel (e.g., *man* is indicated by /man/ rather than by /măn/). A more recent change is the avoidance of diacritical marks that are used to signify different sounds in other languages. As more people learn more than one language, this change will help to avoid confusion. When teaching, it is often beneficial to use more distinguishing marks than the newer dictionaries do. It allows teacher and student to communicate more easily and clearly. The diacritical conventions used in this book combine those used in Webster's New World Dictionary, Second College Edition, with those necessary for teaching beginning readers to distinguish the orthographic structures and sounds of English.[1]

The three most common diacritical marks are the **long vowel mark** ‾ (also called the **macron**), the **short vowel mark** ˘ (also called the **breve**), and the **schwa** mark ə. The long mark placed over a vowel signifies that it is to be pronounced just as it sounds when we recite the alphabet:

ā as in *ate*	ē as in *evil*	ī as in *ice*
ō as in *open*	ū as in *use* or in *flute*	ȳ as in *cry*

The short mark changes the vowel sounds as follows:

ă as in *apple*	ĕ as in *elephant*	ĭ as in *igloo*
ŏ as in *on*	ŭ as in *under*	y̆ as in *gym*

The schwa mark represents the glossed-over, indistinct vowel sound that is in the unaccented or unstressed syllable of a multisyllabic word:

ə as in *ago*	ə as in *happen*	ə as in *legible*
ə as in *common*	ə as in *suggest*	ə as in *syzygy*

The other diacritical marks used in this book are shown in Table 1.

---

[1]Teachers tend to resist making changes in their materials once they are comfortable with a particular set. It really doesn't matter which marks are used to teach decoding, as long as they distinguish among the necessary sounds. It is, however, an added burden on the learner if he or she has to learn an entirely different set of symbols to use the dictionary. Another problem is that dictionaries published by different companies are not all the same. Good teachers will temper their consistency with a little flexibility and will introduce a dictionary pronunciation guide when their students are ready for it.

MARK	SOUND
ô	*s<u>aw</u>, c<u>augh</u>t*
ôr	*sh<u>or</u>t, f<u>or</u>ce*
är	*<u>ar</u>c, f<u>ar</u>*
ʉr	*f<u>er</u>n, sh<u>ir</u>t, c<u>ur</u>b*
öi	*<u>oi</u>l, b<u>oy</u>*
o͞o	*m<u>oo</u>n, thr<u>ough</u>*
o͝o	*b<u>oo</u>k*
ou	*<u>ou</u>t, cr<u>ow</u>d*

Diacritical marks

Table 1

Now that the beginning notes about conventions are finished, we can start working on the definitions and concepts needed as background knowledge to teach the code of written English. The exercises in this book are intended to help you, the reader, understand the phonics and orthographic structure of the English language. Some of the exercises are also useful for teaching these concepts to emerging readers. Of course, emerging readers spend many, many hours, spread over several years, learning and applying these concepts. Gaining fluency with the definitions and concepts will take practice spread over time. As you are learning a new definition or concept, applying it to the words you see on billboards, packages, etc. will provide extra practice during times that are not being used for more important activities.

⟨◌⊠◌⊠◌⊠◌⊠◌⊠◌⊠◌⊠◌⊠◌⊠◌⊠◌⊠◌⟩

II

Vowels and Consonants

◨◇◨

The twenty-six letters of the English alphabet can be organized in many ways. For decoding, they are divided (loosely) into two groups; vowels compose the smaller group, consonants the larger.

Notation: In this book, "v" is used as a generic vowel symbol to show that any vowel may be used in a particular combination of letters. Whenever the context might allow this abbreviation to be confused with the letter *v* itself, the generic symbol is underlined. For instance, *ve* means any vowel followed by an *e*, whereas *ve* means the letter *v* with the letter *e*. Similarly, "c" is used as a generic consonant; when used in conjunction with other letters, it is underlined to indicate that any consonant may be used in its place. Thus, *cl* means any consonant followed by an *l*. Try reading these examples:

ve, cr, cle, cy, vl, vi

Did you say "vowel-e, consonant-r, consonant-l-e, c-y, vowel-l, v-i" to yourself? Good; you understand this notational device.

⬦⬦⬦ Vowels ⬦⬦⬦

> **vowel** [*noun*] (1) a speech sound made by the relatively free movement of air through the mouth, usually forming the main sound of a syllable; or (2) a letter that represents such a sound.

The vowels are *a*, *e*, *i*, *o*, and *u*. The letter *y* sometimes substitutes for *i* and is a vowel when it does so. Likewise, the letter *w* sometimes substitutes

7

for *u* and is considered to be a vowel when it does so; in fact, some people teach that the vowels include *w*. The difference between *y* and *w*, however, is that *y* appears as the only vowel in many syllables (e.g., *syll-*, *gym*, *why*), whereas *w* never appears as a vowel all by itself. When *w* is used as a vowel, it always follows *a*, *e*, or *o* (e.g., *paw*, *new*, *grow*). For this reason, many people do not consider it a vowel. In this book *w* is not called a vowel, except in vowel-team syllables, when it is a substitute for *u*.[1] (Vowel-team syllables are discussed in Chapter III.)

⟨⟩ Single Vowels

When only one vowel appears in a syllable, it is called a **single vowel**. The single vowels all have a variety of sounds depending on the syllable structure, the stress or accent pattern, and the origin of the word. Descriptions of the long, short, and schwa sounds, with exemplifying words, appear on page 5.

Exercise 2.1   Complete the worksheet MARKING THE VOWELS WITH 'V,' on page 9.

⟨⟩ Vowel Teams

A **vowel team** is a combination of two or three vowels, or of a vowel and one or more consonants, that is associated with one or more specific single sounds or sound units. For example, *ay* has the sound /ā/; *ea* has the sounds /ē/, /ĕ/, and /ā/; *igh* has the sound /ī/; *old* has the sound /ōld/. The phrase "vowel team" is an example of vocabulary not traditionally used in texts on teaching reading. Texts on reading often call some (but not all) of these vowel clusters "digraphs" or "diphthongs," depending on their sounds. A **digraph** is a grouping of two or three letters that produces a single sound, such as *ee* in *see*; a **diphthong** is a complex sound made by gliding from one vowel sound to another within the same syllable (e.g., *boy*, *out*).[2]

---

[1] Dually, *u* sometimes has the consonant sound of the *w*, as when it is combined with *q* (*quick* ⇒ /kwĭk/) or in the word *suave*.

[2] Strictly speaking, the prefix *di-* limits *digraph* and *diphthong* to two-letter and two-sound combinations, with the even rarer forms *trigraph* and *triphthong* required for triple letters and triple sounds, respectively. However, many reading textbooks use *digraph* and *diphthong* to distinguish between two different *types* of sound patterns, regardless of the number of letters or sounds involved. The almost unbearable complexity of this terminology makes it virtually useless as a teaching tool.

MARKING THE VOWELS WITH 'V'

a   e   i   o   u

Put a 'v' above each vowel.

<u>Examples</u>:   ǎ   c   ě   ǔ   h   b   ǐ   o   z

- -

a   o   g   a   e   s   a   u   e   l   o   i   n   e

o   p   e   c   u   a   i   f   n   e   i   u   e   g

a   u   t   b   i   e   l   i   u   o   u   e   j   u

i   g   p   o   a   e   e   p   a   u   n   i   v   u

p   u   i   e   a   o   s   u   b   i   v   e   o   a

a   w   u   e   o   k   l   h   i   a   e   u   o   u

i   p   q   e   o   a   s   a   i   u   b   e   o   u

w   o   i   a   f   u   a   e   u   c   e   u   o   i

o   k   e   g   u   o   i   a   w   u   a   e   c   i

o   e   a   s   b   u   i   a   o   d   o   u   e   i

There are several problems with the traditional digraph/diphthong classification. One problem is that the pronunciation of vowels depends significantly on regional dialect. (For example, speakers from the southern states and from "Down-East" Maine tend to use more diphthongs than people from other parts of the country.) Another problem is that a single vowel sometimes may be sounded as a diphthong, depending on which *consonant* follows it. Perhaps the clearest example of pronouncing a single vowel by gliding from one vowel sound to another occurs when the vowel is followed by *l*. For instance, if you say the word *bale*, you will hear yourself say a second vowel sound as you glide from the /ā/ sound to the /l/. A third problem arises from the fact that a single grapheme, such as *ow*, can have both a digraph sound (/ō/ as in *snow*) and a diphthong sound (/ou/ as in *cow*). Since the only way to distinguish between digraphs and diphthongs is to listen to the sounds of words being spoken, and since those sounds depend both on dialect and on vowel-consonant combinations, it follows that classifying vowel teams as digraphs or diphthongs is a changeable process which depends on the speaker, not on the printed grapheme. (This probably accounts for the fact that the listings of digraphs and diphthongs differ from one set of phonics materials to another.)

When teaching or learning about vowel teams, the most important principles to keep in mind are these:

- Students need to learn only enough vocabulary to facilitate effective student ⇔ teacher communication.

- Students should be taught that some groupings of vowels or of vowels and consonants together represent single sounds or specific sound units, and therefore must be treated as visual units. Thus, for example, *igh* says /ī/ (not some combination of other sounds for the *i*, *g*, and *h*); *oo* has two different single sounds, the more common of which is /o͞o/; and *olk* says /ōk/.

- Teachers should call syllables containing *igh*, *oo*, *olk*, or any of the other multiple-letter units by a name that will help students remember that these groupings must be processed as single units, rather than as sequences of separate letters.

The difference between digraphs and diphthongs is not important to beginning readers. Moreover, these two categories do not include the vowel-consonant combinations that have unexpected sounds. Because students must learn the sounds that are particular to every one of these letter units, I have found it easier to teach all of these units using the single classification "vowel team," without other distinguishing vocabulary. In fact, the sounds and use of the vowel teams can be taught without even teaching the students the label "vowel team" itself; nevertheless, it is a helpful term, in that it suggests that the letters work together to form a particular sound unit.

For the purposes of our discussion, it is convenient to consider three different forms in which vowel teams occur in written English:

1. Vowels often appear in clusters within a single syllable. These are the forms that traditionally have been called digraphs and diphthongs (and also trigraphs and triphthongs), as described above.

2. Vowels often appear in combination with a particular consonant or consonants to represent a sound unit that is different from what you would expect if you did not know the particular vowel-consonant combination. For example, the *o* in *old* has the long sound, /ō/, but if you did not know this combination as a special unit, *cold* would look like a syllable structure with a short vowel sound (as we shall see later). There are several of these vowel-consonant combinations that have a sound unit particular to the combination (e.g., *ign* ⇒ /īn/ as in *sign*; *ald* ⇒ /ôld/ as in *bald*; *olt* ⇒ /ōlt/ as in *bolt*).

3. Another somewhat common combination in English is one or two vowels followed by *gh*. The *gh* is *usually* silent (as in *sigh*, *straight*, *eight*, and *though*, but not in *tough*). When decoding, it is much more efficient to process the whole unit (*igh*, *eigh*) than to process the vowel and the *gh* separately.

Because all of these vowel and vowel-consonant combinations must be recognized as visual units, I call all of them vowel teams and I teach them using a common set of specific procedures. (See "Vowel-Team Syllables" in the section on syllable types in Chapter III and the vowel-team pictures for the symbol ⇔ sound correspondences on pages 104–109.)

Perhaps you have noticed that "unit" or "visual unit" has been used where you might expect to see "grapheme," and "sound unit" has been used instead of "phoneme." This is done because a phoneme is a single sound and a grapheme represents a phoneme, so the grapheme–phoneme terminology applies to vowel teams such as *ai* and *ay* that have a single sound, but not to vowel teams such as *old* and *ald* that have sound units composed of a vowel sound and two consonant sounds. Therefore, I use "unit" when "grapheme" does not apply to the entire set of letter combinations being discussed. This distinction is, indeed, precise enough to be called "picky" and I would *never* bother children with it. When teaching, I use the terms "letter," "letters," and "sound," which work just fine.

Exercise 2.2   Complete the six worksheets, IDENTIFYING v-VOWEL
TEAMS IN SYLLABLES, on pages 13–18. These worksheets
are very easy. For most effective learning, you should complete two or three rows at a time, spacing your practice
over several days. Naming the letters as you arc them will
also help you to learn the units. (There is no worksheet for
u-vowel teams because there are only two of them, *ue* and
ui, neither of which is used very often. These are learned
easily enough without a worksheet.)

Exercise 2.3   Memorize the vowel-team pictures in Appendix A (pages
104–109) by filling in blank pictures until you can reproduce
them correctly from memory and know the sounds of each
vowel team.

⊗ Vowels Followed by "R"

When a vowel or vowel team is followed by an *r*, the sound of the vowel is
said to be **r-controlled**. In this book, the vowels followed by *r* are called
vowel-r units (**vr**). The section on syllable types presents a discussion of
the vr syllables (pages 49–53), and the vowel-r picture in Appendix A (the
star on page 109) lists the symbol ⇔ sound correspondences for these units.

Exercise 2.4   Complete the worksheets, IDENTIFYING VOWEL-R-CLOSED
UNITS IN SYLLABLES and IDENTIFYING VOWEL-R VOWEL
TEAMS IN SYLLABLES, on pages 19 and 20.

Exercise 2.5   Memorize the vowel-r picture (the star on page 109) by
filling in blank pictures until you can reproduce the vowel-r
picture correctly from memory and know the sound of each
vowel-r unit.

IDENTIFYING A-VOWEL TEAMS IN SYLLABLES

ai   wa   qua   au   all   alm

Arc under the a-vowel team in each word.

<u>Examples</u>:　main   maul   stall   calm   wash   squash

- -

chain   wash   squat   all   Paul   calm   swamp

squab   balm   haul   drain   ball   squad   pail

want   fault   tall   palm   water   alms   Spain

small   quaff   cause   psalm   aim   fraud   all

quantity   fall   watch   train   gauze   becalm

squash   maul   all   faint   call   swap   haunt

quash   paint   pause   mall   twaddle   calmly

squander   ail   sauce   wasp   stall   fail

quad   balm   swan   squash   vault   ball   main

calm   launch   swab   palm   all   braid   balm

want   squat   hall   balm   jail   caulk   swash

IDENTIFYING A-VOWEL TEAMS IN SYLLABLES

ay   aw   augh   alt   alk   ald

Arc under the a-vowel team in each word.

<u>Examples:</u>   pay   draw   caught   salt   walk   bald

- -

say   saw   malt   aught   talk   bald   caught

bay   asphalt   chalk   shawl   ribald   basalt

clay   flaw   scald   taught   talk   spray

stalk   naughty   halt   draw   piebald   stray

bald   daughter   awning   salt   ray   emerald

naught   gray   Balkan   law   cobalt   scald

day   chalk   caught   malt   dawn   Kay   talk

spawn   pay   bald   fraught   play   Falkland

slay   exalt   yawn   haughty   bald   drawn

tray   scald   lay   taught   balk   asphalt

day   stalk   paw   halt   caught   malt   fray

IDENTIFYING I-VOWEL TEAMS IN SYLLABLES

ie (ye)   ind   igh   ign

Arc under the i-vowel team in each word.

<u>Examples:</u> piece   Skye   night   kind   align

- -

piece   thigh   kind   chief   sign   sight   pie

align   vie   mind   assign   Skye   tight   rind

grieve   high   find   benign   shriek   sign

wield   sigh   blind   fie   grieves   align

grind   field   bright   bind   liege   knight

niece   benign   wright   Skye   sign   hind

brief   fief   slight   vie   remind   fiend

sigh   rind   pie   nigh   right   frieze

grieve   grind   yield   find   plight   Skye

align   rind   tight   grieve   high   mind

sight   pie   align   sign   rind   Skye   tight

IDENTIFYING E-VOWEL TEAMS IN SYLLABLES

ee   ea   ei(ey)   eigh   eu(ew)

Arc under the e-vowel team in each word.

Examples: see   feint   they   eight   feud   pea

- -

sleep   beat   grey   sewer   feint   sleuth

sleigh   drew   cheese   peach   aweigh   feud

weave   they   newt   eight   breath   receive

eulogy   steep   shrewd   freight   crease

weed   stew   beige   sleuth   sleeve   threw

weight   feat   cheek   hewn   wheel   threat

whey   eutrophic   prey   stealth   reindeer

tease   either   new   Greek   clean   they

feud   sleigh   neither   lease   wheeze   flew

survey   whew   apartheid   deuce   counterfeit

ease   prey   leapt   forfeit   neutral   obey

IDENTIFYING O-VOWEL TEAMS IN SYLLABLES

oo   old   oi   oy   olk   olt

Arc under the o-vowel team in each word.

Examples: soon   gold   joist   Troy   folk   bolt

- -

soon   gold   joist   Troy   folk   bolt   wool

noise   molt   Roy   old   moose   Polk   colt

joy   told   look   yolk   volt   point   boy

stood   polk   oil   jolt   Boyd   old   mood

yolk   sold   molt   toil   too   ploy   folk

scold   groove   colt   oomph   soy   volt   folk

voice   Lloyd   foist   bolt   fold   room   boy

swoop   molt   folk   zoom   choice   joy   jolt

old   volt   oink   toy   cold   coo   colt   polk

spoil   goose   destroy   hoof   bolt   Royce

yolk   join   snooze   mold   coy   jolt   ooze

IDENTIFYING O-VOWEL TEAMS IN SYLLABLES

ou   ow   oll   ost   oa   oe

Arc under the o-vowel team in each word.

<u>Examples:</u>   shout   cow   loll   host   boat   shoe

- -

shout   cow   loll   host   boat   shoe   ouch

knoll   poach   down   trout   doe   most   doll

browse   post   mouse   poll   rouge   groan

foe   cost   doubt   troll   know   whoa   Joe

soul   oat   floe   grow   post   roll   loath

out   toe   roam   doll   ground   town   lost

woe   loathe   scroll   post   how   doe   scout

knoll   ghost   frown   froe   lost   rouse

coast   vow   throe   loll   Joe   group   soap

roll   frost   oak   lounge   host   stroll

shoe   blow   coat   most   doll   below   toe

IDENTIFYING VOWEL-R-CLOSED UNITS IN SYLLABLES

ar   er   ir   or   ur   war   wor

Arc under the <u>v</u>r or w<u>v</u>r unit in each word.

<u>Examples</u>: jar   orb   fur   perk   firm   word   warm

- -

car   skirt   worth   sort   large   blurb   herd

work   arm   warm   yard   or   sir   dwarf   Herb

morn   hurl   worse   harm   term   ward   swirl

warp   start   burst   cork   starve   worst

work   arm   bird   her   horse   worst   harsh

twerp   short   urge   world   fork   part   orb

thwart   burst   curl   warm   perk   dwarf

ward   first   curb   torque   word   firm   war

charm   slur   her   twirl   warm   merge   York

fur   worst   jar   fern   force   fir   burn

worth   bird   warm   yarn   perk   dwarf   or

IDENTIFYING VOWEL-R VOWEL TEAMS IN SYLLABLES

air   ear   eer   ier   oar   oor   our

Arc under the vr-vowel team in each word.

Examples: fair   courtesy   yearn   board   pier

- -

stair   veneer   dreary   tour   poor   tier

our   coarse   Montpelier   Europe   fairly

journal   eerie   pierce   whippoorwill

uproar   four   prairie   neuron   Moore   cheer

earth   pier   solitaire   courage   mutineer

our   footwear   hoard   racecourse   search

horsehair   veer   amateur   repair   fierce

coarse   earnest   boar   reindeer   affair

source   learn   oar   volunteer   cashier

tear   pasteurize   pearl   despair   devour

gear   neurology   midair   pioneer   moor

⬦⬦ Consonants ⬦⬦

consonant [*noun; from the Latin verb consonare, to sound along with, to harmonize*] (1) a speech sound made by partially or completely blocking the vocal air stream; or (2) a letter that represents such a sound.

The consonants are the letters that are not vowels. (When *y* is not a vowel, it is a consonant.) Most of the consonants and consonant teams have only one sound, though a few have multiple sounds (e.g., *c* ⇒ /k/ and /s/). (For a list of these grapheme ⇒ phoneme correspondences, see pages 97–100 in Appendix A.)

⬦⬦ Single Consonants

When one consonant appears alone in a syllable (i.e., with no consonant right next to it), it is called a **single consonant**. Thus, *mop*, *sit*, *time*, and *seed* each have two single consonants; *velvet* has two single consonants in each syllable.

Exercise 2.6   Complete the worksheet, MARKING VOWELS WITH 'V' AND CONSONANTS WITH 'C,' on page 22.

Exercise 2.7   Practice giving the sounds for the single consonants, using the grapheme ⇒ phoneme correspondences on pages 97 and 98.

⬦⬦ Single-Sound Consonant Teams

Often two and sometimes three consonants appear together and have a single sound. For example, *ph* has the sound /f/ and *-ck* has the sound /k/. Some of these graphemes have traditionally been called digraphs, but not all the graphemes that have only one sound were included in the group called digraphs, and they don't fit the consonant-blend category (described below). When teaching, it is easier to have a single category for all consonant teams that represent individual phonemes, so they will be called **single-sound consonant teams (SSCT)** in this book. Notice that some single-sound consonant teams have a silent letter (e.g., *kn-*, *gn-*, *pn-*, *wr-*, *-mb*).

MARKING VOWELS WITH 'V' AND CONSONANTS WITH 'C'

a   e   i   o   u

Put a 'V' above each vowel and a 'C' above each consonant.

Examples:
```
      V    C    V    V    C    V    V    C
      a    c    e    u    h    i    o    z
```

- -

```
a   o   g   a   p   s   a   v   e   l   b   i   n   e

d   o   e   c   d   a   i   f   u   s   i   t   e   g

a   u   t   b   n   e   l   i   u   k   w   e   j   u

i   g   p   o   n   r   e   p   a   u   n   i   v   u

p   u   n   b   a   o   s   j   b   i   v   e   s   q

a   w   u   p   o   k   l   h   m   a   e   g   n   u

i   p   q   d   o   r   s   a   i   t   b   e   v   u

w   o   i   z   f   h   a   e   d   c   u   q   o   v

o   k   e   g   f   r   i   a   w   u   b   e   c   i

o   f   a   s   b   c   i   a   p   d   o   r   s   d
```

There are two three-letter teams that some people find confusing:

-tch and *-dge*

Because the /t/ and /ch/ sounds and also the /d/ and /j/ sounds are formed with almost exactly the same tongue, lip, and mouth positions, it may seem as though the /t/ and the /d/ are pronounced separately from the /ch/ and the /j/. However, there is no difference between the /ch/ sounds at the end of *such* and *crutch*, nor between the /j/ sounds at the end of *cage* and *badge*. Therefore, these graphemes are properly considered to be single-sound consonant teams.

Some of the units that have traditionally been included in this group really have a blended sound that is quite different from the blend of sounds that the individual letters have in isolation. Since the blended sound is a sound that is unique to the team, it makes sense to include these units in the category of single-sound consonant teams:

- The consonant *q* is almost always followed by the vowel *u*. (There are some names that do not follow this convention.) The *u* does not act as a vowel in this team; the sound of the team at the beginning of words is /kw/, with the *u* having the same sound that the consonant *w* has. The *qu* must be learned and recognized as a consonant team so that the *u* is not confused with a vowel. For example, in *quick*, the *qu* is a consonant team; the only vowel is *i*.

  The *qu* could be considered a blend instead of a single-sound consonant team. Its label is not as important as the fact that the *u*, when put with *q*, is given the sound of *w*, rather than its usual sound, making *u* a consonant, not a vowel, in this case.

  A related consonant team involving *q* occurs at the ends of some French-derivative words, where *-que* says /k/ (as in *torque* or *plaque*).

- The *-ng* and *-nk* units (as in *sing* and *sank* have a different sound for *n* than would be heard in a blend (such as the *nd* in *hand*). The tongue changes position and produces a much more nasal sound for /ng/ and /nk/ than for /nd/.

Exercise 2.8   Complete the four worksheets, FINDING SINGLE-SOUND CONSONANT TEAMS IN WORDS, on pages 24–27.

Exercise 2.9   Practice giving the sounds for the single-sound consonant teams, using the grapheme ⇒ phoneme correspondences on pages 98–100.

FINDING SINGLE-SOUND CONSONANT TEAMS IN WORDS

qu   ck   ff   ll   ss   zz

Arc under every single-sound consonant team.

<u>Examples:</u>   pack   quill   quit   tiff   mass   jazz

- -

sass	Jill	pick	Zack	quip	jazz	miff
pack	quiz	quill	kiss	hill	hack	pass
rack	tiff	sill	fill	lack	Cass	wick
miss	Matt	mill	sack	quack	quip	back
jazz	riff	fizz	pill	tack	Rick	hiss
mass	lick	miff	quip	bass	quick	hill
rack	tick	hiss	Nick	fizz	pass	ill
tiff	quack	lack	miss	Cass	jazz	back
sick	quip	pack	quit	mill	Zack	sass
fizz	quip	pill	sack	sill	quiz	Jill
pick	quill	fill	quack	tack	hill	bass

FINDING SINGLE-SOUND CONSONANT TEAMS IN WORDS

sh   ch   th   ng   nk

Arc under every single-sound consonant team.

Examples: shin   these   chap   cash   ring   crank

- -

shin   these   chap   cash   ring   crank   bath

cheese   rush   dong   machine   that   sunk

ship   think   moth   chin   shore   lurch   lung

then   ache   mash   munch   oink   three   shush

sang   cheep   bother   thong   rink   shun

choir   wink   shop   march   thank   rung   ink

shell   church   north   slang   hunk   mesh

bring   shrunk   oath   song   sink   short

this   chill   sank   slung   rank   breath

Chris   tong   slink   plush   thin   shape

king   rather   dunk   sheep   chant   hung

FINDING SINGLE-SOUND CONSONANT TEAMS IN WORDS

wh   ph   gh-   -tch   -dge

Arc under every single-sound consonant team.

Examples: when   phone   ghost   catch   budge

- -

when   phone   ghost   catch   budge   whale

graph   witch   siphon   who   fudge   ghoul

ditch   whistle   phantom   edge   Ghana   match

why   bridge   Mitch   ledge   phrase   synch

badge   crutch   ghetto   wedge   whirl   ghost

witch   Ralph   smudge   wheel   ridge   catch

wheat   Phyllis   pledge   ghastly   grudge

lymph   whey   Ghana   pitch   sphinx   dredge

sorghum   white   edge   triumph   retch   whorl

wedge   fetch   judge   whiz   gopher   gherkin

cadge   wretch   hedge   elephant   whet   hitch

FINDING SINGLE-SOUND CONSONANT TEAMS IN WORDS

kn   gn   wr   -mb

Arc under every single-sound consonant team.

Examples: knit   gnarl   writ   bomb

- -

knit   gnarl   writ   bomb   know   womb   wreath

knot   climb   gnaw   wrinkle   kneel   lamb

gnat   wring   knell   comb   write   knife

dumb   wreck   gnu   jamb   wrong   knave   gnash

limb   numb   knead   wrath   gnat   wrist   knot

knight   wreck   gnu   wren   knit   plumb   tomb

knock   wrap   thumb   knack   gnarl   crumb

wraith   knapsack   gnome   kneel   wrack   knob

gnome   wrestle   limb   knit   plumb   gnu

wretch   knee   succumb   writ   gnash   write

comb   gnome   wrist   climb   know   jamb   gnu

⬦ Consonant Blends

When two or more consonants appear together and you hear each sound
that each consonant would normally make, the consonant team is called a
consonant blend. For example, *blend* has two consonant blends: *bl*, for
which you hear the sounds for *b* and *l*, and *nd*, for which you hear the sounds
for both *n* and *d*.

There are a few groups of consonants that combine a single-sound consonant team with a single consonant (e.g., *shr* and *thr*). These groups are
often called **consonant clusters**. The term "cluster" does not provide any
way of distinguishing these groups from the other groups, and it seems not
to matter if they are separated from the category of consonant blends when
they are taught. They can be considered blends if the single-sound consonant team is considered to be one unit and the single consonant is considered
to be another unit, with each unit making its usual sound. Again, the labels
are not as important as knowing how to explain these groups when they are
taught.

If the consonant clusters are included with the consonant blends, then the
consonant units can be summarized by dividing them into three categories,
each with a label that indicates its characteristic feature:

- single consonants are consonants appearing alone;

- single-sound consonant teams are two or more consonants appearing
  as a team that have a single sound (or a sound unique to the letter
  unit);

- consonant blends are two or more consonants appearing as a team in
  which each letter unit retains its usual sound.

Exercise 2.10 Complete the exercise sheet, SORTING SINGLE-SOUND CON-
SONANT TEAMS AND BLENDS, on page 29. (Answers are on
page 129.)

Exercise 2.11 Take a page from a magazine, newspaper, or book and
highlight in one color all the single-sound consonant teams.
Highlight in a different color all the consonant blends.

Exercise 2.12 Practice saying the sounds for the consonant blends identified in Exercises 2.10 and 2.11. Do the same for the single-
sound consonant teams.

SORTING SINGLE-SOUND CONSONANT TEAMS AND BLENDS

The single-sound consonant teams (SSCT) and blends in the words below have been printed in bold type. Write each SSCT in a column labeled SSCTs and write each blend in a column labeled BLENDS. The first four have been done for you.

bl a **ck** ✓ **squ** id la **mb** ✓ **wh** i **zz** **spl** i nt **sm** e **lt** **gr** a **ph**

gn a **sh** **wr** i st **fr** i **sk** **kn** ave **th** i nk **spr** u **ng**

thr ice **pn** euma **cl** u **tch** **shr** ike **str** oke **scr** u **nch**

sw i **ft** **cr** y **pt** **ch** i **mp** **ps** alm **tr** i **ll** **pl** e **dge** **qu** it

SSCTs			BLENDS	
ck	___		bl	___
mb	___		squ	___
___	___		___	___
___	___		___	___
___	___		___	___
___	___		___	___
___	___		___	___
___	___		___	___
___	___		___	___
___	___		___	___
___	___		___	___
___	___		___	___

◈ Hard and Soft C and G

The sound of the letter *c* is controlled by the letter following it. When *c* is followed by a consonant (other than *h*) or by *a*, *o*, or *u*, it has the sound /k/; when it is followed by *e* or *i* (or *y*), it has the sound /s/. For example, listen to the sound of *c* in *class*, *cat*, *cot*, and *cut*; then listen to the sound of *c* in *city*, *cyst*, and *cellar*. /k/ is often called the **hard sound**, and /s/ is often called the **soft sound**. This pattern is extremely regular for *c*.

The letter *g* follows the same pattern, with the hard sound represented by /g/ and the soft sound represented by /j/, but its behavior is not nearly as regular. Listen to the sound of *g* in *glass*, *gate*, *goat*, and *gust*; then listen to its sound in *general*, *gym*, and *giant*.[3] Here are some common words that don't follow the pattern: *get*, *give*, *gear*, *gill*, *girl*.

Exercise 2.13   Complete these worksheets, which appear on pages 32–34:
  − C AND G BEFORE A AND E
  − C AND G BEFORE O AND I
  − C AND G BEFORE U AND Y

Exercise 2.14   Take or copy a page from a magazine, newspaper, or book and mark it as follows:
  − put "K" above every hard *c*;
  − put "S" above every soft *c*;
  − put "G" above every hard *g*;
  − put "J" above every soft *g*.

◈ Y as a Consonant and as a Vowel

The rule for distinguishing when *y* is a vowel and when it is a consonant is simple and virtually absolute:

> The letter *y* is a consonant when it is the first letter of a syllable that has more than one letter. If *y* is anywhere else in the syllable, it is a vowel.

---

[3]This pattern can be taught without ever using the terms "hard" and "soft" for the sounds. However, it often helps students to pair the unvoiced /k/ and the voiced /g/, which are produced in the same way; these sounds can be called either "hard" or "the sound that goes with *a*, *o*, *u*, and consonants." Similarly, the term "soft" can be replaced by "the sound that goes with *e*, *i*, and *y*."

Thus, *y* is a consonant in *yes, yam, yell, yellow, yogurt,* and *banyan*; it is a vowel in *gym, my, cycle,* and *baby.* When *y* is the only letter in the syllable, it is a vowel because every syllable has to have a vowel; that is, *y* cannot be a consonant all by itself.

Exercise 2.15 Complete the worksheets, Y AS A CONSONANT and Y AS A VOWEL, on pages 35 and 36.

Exercise 2.16 Take a page from a magazine, newspaper, or book and highlight in one color all *y*'s that are consonants. Highlight in a different color all *y*'s that are vowels.

C AND *G* BEFORE *A* AND *E*

1.   ***C* says /k/ when it comes before *a*.**
***C* says /s/ when it comes before *e*.**

Put *k* or *s* above the *c*.   <u>Examples</u>: $\overset{K}{\text{ca}}$ $\overset{S}{\text{ce}}$

ca	ce	ce	ca	ca	ca	ce	ce	ca
ce	ce	ca	ca	ce	ce	ce	ca	ce
ce	ca	ce	ca	ca	ca	ce	ce	ca
ca	ce	ce	ca	ce	ca	ca	ce	ca

2.   ***G* says /g/ when it comes before *a*.**
***G* usually says /j/ before *e*.**

Put *g* or *j* above the g.   <u>Examples</u>: $\overset{g}{\text{ga}}$ $\overset{j}{\text{ge}}$

ga	ga	ge	ge	ga	ge	ga	ga	ge
ga	ge	ge	ge	ga	ge	ge	ga	ge
ga	ga	ge	ge	ge	ga	ga	ga	ge
ge	ga	ga	ge	ge	ga	ge	ga	ga

C AND *G* BEFORE *O* AND *I*

1. **C says /k/ when it comes before *o*.**
   C says /s/ when it comes before *i*.

   Put *k* or *s* above the c.   Examples: K   S
                                         co   ci

co	ci	ci	co	co	co	ci	ci	co
ci	ci	co	co	ci	ci	ci	co	ci
ci	co	ci	co	co	co	ci	ci	co
co	ci	ci	co	ci	co	co	ci	co

2. **G says /g/ when it comes before *o*.**
   G usually says /j/ before *i*.

   Put *g* or *j* above the g.   Examples: g   j
                                         go   gi

go	go	gi	gi	go	gi	go	go	gi
go	gi	gi	gi	go	gi	gi	go	gi
go	go	gi	go	gi	gi	go	go	go
gi	go	go	gi	gi	go	gi	go	go

C AND *G* BEFORE *U* AND *Y*

1.   *C* says /k/ when it comes before *u*.
      C says /s/ when it comes before *y*.

      Put *k* or *s* above the *c*.   Examples: $\overset{k}{cu}$ $\overset{s}{cy}$

cu	cy	cy	cu	cu	cu	cy	cy	cu
cy	cy	cu	cu	cy	cy	cy	cu	cy
cy	cu	cy	cu	cu	cu	cy	cy	cu
cu	cu	cy	cu	cy	cy	cy	cu	cu

2.   *G* says /g/ when it comes before *u*.
      G usually says /j/ before *y*.

      Put *g* or *j* above the *g*.   Examples: $\overset{g}{gu}$ $\overset{j}{gy}$

gu	gu	gy	gy	gu	gy	gu	gu	gy
gu	gy	gy	gy	gu	gy	gy	gu	gu
gy	gu	gy	gy	gy	gu	gu	gu	gy
gy	gu	gu	gy	gy	gu	gy	gu	gu

Y AS A CONSONANT

Y is a consonant when it is the first letter of a word or syllable. Put a 'c' above every y that is a consonant.

Examples:
   ᶜyap   ᶜyell   ᶜyear   by   ᶜyet   rhyme   ᶜyou

- -

yet   yoke   yard   yellow   why   yearn   yak

rhyme   year   you   yelp   fly   yip   syllable

young   yours   year   yard   merry   yen   buy

yell   sly   York   yacht   hay   yoke   yucca

rhyme   yodel   yen   baby   cycle   yearn   yolk

yuletide   play   yeast   yap   ply   yew   yell

Yankee   syllable   yarrow   yet   yam   yodel

yeast   yell   thyme   yard   yield   yearn   cry

youthful   Yonkers   yowl   stray   yip   yam

yelp   yawn   yeast   yes   yellow   candy   you

yucca   pry   yam   Yiddish   silly   say   yowl

Y AS A VOWEL

Y is a vowel when it comes <u>after</u> the first letter of a word or syllable. Put a 'v' above every y that is a vowel.

<u>Examples:</u> rh**y**me c**y**cle cr**y** **y**ou pla**y** bo**y**

- -

sly stray tyke yet why rhyme yellow

ray pry gym city fly yearn myth try

cycle cherry yucca yes byte buy sorry

yam city sly cypress Clyde spry young

sylph buy thyme year pray psycho my

xylophone type yet my Jayne royal

yeast ply dry Tyson play yours myth

city fry berry sylph yawn cycle sly

gray yodel cry stray yelp foyer buy

type tyrant symbol yearn symptom pyre

dye syrup yep cymbal cynic baby you

III

Syllables

syllable [*noun*] (1) in a spoken language, any one of the basic units
of uninterrupted sound that can be used to make up words; or
(2) in a written language, any letter or symbol grouping that
represents a spoken syllable.

The letters of the English alphabet are the symbols used in the written code
by which we communicate. The letters—or more precisely, the graphemes—
represent the individual sounds of the language. Because the letters of the
alphabet represent the individual sounds of English, we call English an "alphabetic" language. Another major component of the code is the syllable
structure of our language. Before examining the syllable structure of English,
it may be helpful to understand the advantages of languages that represent
sounds and syllables by symbols over languages that do not. Let us take a
brief look at some history.

The first written communication systems were pictures that represented
entire events (such as the famous pictures in the cave in Lescaux, France).
For more precise communication, pictures began to represent smaller units
of ideas, and then individual items and words. These pictures are called
logograms, and the languages that use them are called **logographic**. Although these logographic systems were easy to interpret, as languages added
more and more words they quickly became cumbersome because of the large
number of pictures needed. (Japanese and Chinese are logographic, as well
as syllabic, languages; Japanese has several thousand logograms in addition
to its syllabic symbols.) Moreover, representation of words that do not refer
to concrete things or activities requires unique symbols. With the addition

of the more abstract symbols needed to represent words without concrete meanings, written communication was no longer so easy to use or interpret. People had to learn what a symbol meant, and if they wanted to communicate in writing, they had to learn which symbols to use for the abstract words.

The notion of representing words by units of sound (instead of representing the meanings of the words) had a major advantage, in that the same symbol could be used to represent the same sound unit in every word containing it. Since syllables of words are distinct sound units that people hear easily, it was natural for writing systems to evolve into **syllabic** systems, written languages in which a different symbol is used to represent the sound of each distinct syllable. This was particularly natural in the languages that had very simple syllables made up of a consonant sound plus a vowel sound (e.g., *ma, mu, ti, po*). Not only did this reduce the number of symbols needed, but abstract ideas and names could be represented just as easily as "dog," "horse," or "house" because the sounds, not the objects, were being represented. The disadvantage, of course, was that the symbols no longer represented concrete things that were readily understood.

The syllabic system, where a symbol represents an entire syllable, may have a major advantage over a logographic system in languages that have simple syllables, but it loses this advantage for languages that have more, as well as more complex, syllables. English has an estimated 5,000 distinct syllables; learning to use and write that many different symbols would indeed be difficult. The development of the **alphabetic** system, in which the symbols represent the simplest individual sounds of the language, made it possible to represent even languages with large syllabaries and the most complex syllables by a small set of symbols.

Alphabetic writing systems reduce the number of symbols to be memorized to a manageable task, one that can be learned by most people who speak the language. This lessened memory demand is an enormous advantage of an alphabetic writing system, but there are related disadvantages. Since the symbols represent individual sounds instead of syllables, the reader/writer must learn not only the symbols themselves, but also the symbol patterns that create the syllables. And, as is the case with syllabic systems, the symbols are abstract, in that they represent sounds, rather than concrete items. These disadvantages are magnified for English because it is not a perfectly alphabetic system. In a perfectly alphabetic system, each sound would be represented by one and only one letter. However, as we saw in Chapter II, many of the sounds in English are represented by several different graphemes, and many graphemes have more than one sound.

Most children who grow up in the United States learn to decode the symbols and patterns of English over a period of four to six or seven years. Some of the learning takes place at home, and some of it takes place at school. Most of these children learn the sounds for the letters by being told explicitly that a letter has a particular sound or sounds. Sesame Street teaches the sounds in this manner, many parents tell their children the sounds for letters, and many kindergarten and first grade teachers teach these symbol⇔sound relationships to children. Most children who become good readers do not have to be taught the syllable structure of English directly. They learn the syllable structure by memorizing a basic set of sight words[1] and then using these words to figure out how to pronounce other words with similar-looking patterns. For example, children might memorize the word *look* and then use this word and their knowledge of the sounds for the letters to decode *book*, *took*, and *cook*. Likewise, they might memorize *take* and *came*, and then use this knowledge to figure out *lake*, *bake*, *same*, *name*, *tame*, and *game*. Soon they would realize that they should use the long vowel sounds (the name of the letter) when they see a word that has one vowel followed by one consonant followed by an *e*; furthermore, they would realize that the *e* is silent. When the patterns are learned in this way, they are understood implicitly, rather than explicitly. As a result, readers who can use these patterns effectively often can't explain them clearly.

For many children and adults, learning to decode these patterns is not at all easy. Many people do not memorize the symbol ⇔ sound relationships easily, do not learn to recognize the patterns of the syllables easily, and do not learn to manipulate the sounds within the syllables easily. Most of these people can learn to decode English if they are taught the sounds and syllable patterns directly and are trained to listen for and manipulate the separate sounds of the syllables they speak. Teachers, therefore, must have an *explicit* understanding of the syllable structure of English in order to be able to teach it to *all* their students.

In the teaching of reading it has been customary to say that a syllable is a word or word part that has one and only one vowel sound. Indeed, it is the vowel sound, by itself or combined with consonant sounds, which gives that part of the word its single, uninterrupted sounding of the voice. But this is only the auditory part of the process. When reading, we begin with the visual process by looking at the printed letters. The visual part of the process requires the reader to recognize the syllable—the printed unit which

---

[1] A **sight word** is a word that is recognized so automatically that the reader does not have to focus on the sounds of the individual letters.

produces that single, uninterrupted sound of the voice—and to know which sounds are to be produced in forming that syllable. Thus, an understanding of syllable structure is required of the reader of English.

Exercise 3.1   Complete the worksheet, IDENTIFYING SYLLABLES (ALL VOWELS), on page 41.

⊗⊗⊗ The Six Syllable Types ⊗⊗⊗

In English it is customary to define and label six different syllable categories, each with its own set of pronunciation rules. As these labels and rules have been taught to beginning readers over the years, some labels have remained consistent (e.g., closed syllable), and some labels have varied with different programs (e.g., silent-e vs. magic-e). The labels used in these materials have been adopted as a result of many years of work with both children and adults. Rationales are presented to explain why the traditional labels are often less useful in teaching; the traditional labels are also included, so that the reader can refer knowledgeably to other materials.

> **concept** [*noun*] an idea or mental construct, especially one formed
> by generalizing from some specific objects, instances, or events.

In the case of a syllable type, the class of objects includes all of the words and nonword syllables that have the visual characteristics of that syllable. The characteristics or features of the words that distinguish this class of words or nonword syllables from other classes of words constitute the generalized idea of that syllable type. We often call the class of objects a **concept category**. For a more concrete example, think of the concept category 'chair.' If you wanted to define this concept 'chair,' you would need to think of all of the features of the items you call 'chair' that distinguish chairs from other items. These features that distinguish chairs from other things are called the relevant (or distinctive) features; the characteristics that do not matter are called their irrelevant (or nondistinctive) features. Since the syllable structures are presented as concepts in this book and in the teaching materials that are available as a companion to it, they are defined here in terms of relevant (distinctive) features and irrelevant (nondistinctive) features.

IDENTIFYING SYLLABLES (ALL VOWELS)

1. Put a 'V' above every vowel.

2. Arc under every syllable.

Examples: I   cap   eat   ble   cmz

- -

me   a   be   slat   cp   see   blu   eam   rxf

plee   bagrmt   I   gr   wain   light   leave

spl   great   velve   num   vi   mer   grp   tion

u   ck   plo   trio   prsh   fools   nel   x   note

age   eag   plug   tor   mczw   zine   scop   a

ine   shr   mine   brlk   o   mu   veel   ploat   a

vrt   clr   heark   ggrd   I   gew   mere   u   dr

week   pois   shralk   xnmd   wre   incr   jour

poar   k   hier   scien   eer   lour   ness   brig

deer   trt   mill   ou   bi   strength   drght   o

bleak   tame   tion   psg   e   ear   stig   gle

⬦ Closed Syllables (CL)

Examples: *in ask sock truck stretch twelfth on syll- cym-*

Relevant (Distinctive) Features:

1. A closed syllable has one and only one vowel.
2. It ends in a consonant.

Irrelevant (Nondistinctive) Features:

1. The particular vowel that is used does not matter.
2. The particular consonants that are used do not matter, unless the consonant(s) used in conjunction with the vowel form(s) a vowel-team syllable (see page 46) or a vowel-r syllable (see page 49).
3. The number of consonants before the vowel does not matter.
4. The number of consonants after the vowel does not matter, as long as there is at least one.

Exercise 3.2   Complete the worksheet, IDENTIFYING CLOSED SYLLABLES (ALL VOWELS), on page 43.

⬦ Open Syllables (O)

Examples: *no she I a spry mu- pre- e-*

Relevant (Distinctive) Features:

1. An open syllable has one and only one vowel.
2. The vowel is at the end of the syllable.

Irrelevant (Nondistinctive) Features:

1. The particular vowel that is used does not matter.
2. The particular consonants that are used do not matter, except in the cases of the CLE syllables (see page 53) and of *w* before *a*, which forms a vowel-team syllable (see page 46).
3. The number of consonants before the vowel does not matter.

Exercise 3.3   Complete the worksheet, IDENTIFYING OPEN SYLLABLES (ALL VOWELS), on page 44.

IDENTIFYING CLOSED SYLLABLES (ALL VOWELS)

1. Put a 'v' above every vowel.

2. Put a 'c' above every consonant that follows the vowel.

3. Arc under the closed syllables.

Examples:
$$\begin{array}{ccccc} \overset{v\,c}{\underset{\smile}{at}} & \overset{v\,c\,c\,c}{\underset{\smile}{inch}} & \overset{v\,c\,e}{slope} & \overset{v\,c}{\underset{\smile}{cut}} & \overset{v\,c\,c}{\underset{\smile}{rest}} \end{array}$$

- -

cat   stop   ran   tape   in   up   seem   it

not   trim   she   fleck   such   on   well

tree   sack   bring   am   stretch   see   got

truck   step   time   tip   lest   umps   us   a

scram   win   clam   see   at   hop   I   slant

it   use   stumps   cinch   tramp   Tom   be

inch   bend   ranch   end   trot   link   ump

sprain   wrench   camp   to   wet   sleep

hash   pup   notch   pile   ramp   hutch   egg

fly   soft   clan   stuff   use   pun   fast

IDENTIFYING OPEN SYLLABLES (ALL VOWELS)

1.   Put a 'V' above every vowel.

2.   Arc under the open syllables.

Examples: ǎ   bě   wǐsě   trý   Ǐ

- - - - - - - - - - - - - - - - - - -

a   cry   no   tra   mean   e   fro

bi   ask   why   she   plu   o   see

pla   u   chi   home   he   cry   vo

inch   a   I   cu   pre   pea   so

sli   try   aim   o   lu   we   spa

ant   to   sly   cre   u   hi   need

flu   i   ump   ra   rob   le   phy

free   try   mu   cra   cy   an   she

go   sti   my   sea   fro   bu   schi

ice   he   shy   clu   arm   pro   re

by   plea   ri   pnu   go   inch   cla

❖ Magic-E Syllables (ME)

Examples: *ate   ice   tune   slope   strobe   these   -ote   -ine   -ume*

Relevant (Distinctive) Features:

1. A magic-e syllable ends in an *e*.
2. It has one and only one consonant before the ending *e*.
3. It has one and only one vowel before the consonant.

Irrelevant (Nondistinctive) Features:

1. The particular vowel used before the consonant does not matter.
2. The particular consonants used do not matter, except in *vre* units, which might better be called vowel-r-magic-e syllables (see page 51).
3. The number of consonants before the vowel does not matter.

These are often called "silent-e" syllables. The *e* is silent in these syllables, but the final *e* also is silent in many words and syllables that do not have the *vce* structure. For example: *peace* and *noise* have two vowels before the *ce*; *large* has a vowel-r unit before the *ce*; *France* has an extra consonant between the vowel and the *e*. The *e*'s in all of these words are called **marker e's** because they "mark"—or control—something in the word. The *e* in a magic-e syllable controls the vowel sound, making it long. The *e* in these other words does not control the vowel sound, but rather marks some other aspect of the word. (For instance, the final *e* in *peace*, *large*, and *France* makes the *c* and *g* sounds soft.) Most of these other words belong under the categories indicated by their vowel structures. To avoid confusion with the other silent (marker) *e*'s, it is more helpful to call the syllables with the *vce* pattern "magic-e syllables."

Two special cases of marker-e words are worth noting:

- A few words have a single-sound consonant team (usually *th*) between the first vowel and the *e*. These generally have a long vowel sound, as though the SSCT were only one letter. Some examples are:

  bathe, tithe, lathe, scythe, blithe, clothe, butte, tulle

- In English, we never end a word in *v*; we always add an *e*. When words have a -*vve* pattern, the vowel sometimes is short, but more often it is long. The *e* marks the *v* and usually also marks the vowel, as in

  give, live, dive, hive, have, gave, stove

Interestingly, there are very few monosyllabic (i.e., one-syllable) words of the magic-e structure that have the *e* as the first vowel:

Crete, eke, eve, cede, gene, mete, Pete, plebe,

scene, scheme, Steve, Swede, theme, these

In monosyllabic words, the *ee* vowel team is the most common spelling for /ē/ plus a consonant sound, whereas *vce* is the most common spelling pattern for the vowel sounds /ā/, /ī/, /ō/, and /ū/.

Exercise 3.4   Complete the worksheet, IDENTIFYING MAGIC-E SYLLA-BLES (ALL VOWELS), on page 47.

Exercise 3.5   Complete the exercise sheet, SORTING MAGIC-E AND OTHER MARKER-E SYLLABLES, on page 48. (Answers are on page 130.)

◈ Vowel-Team Syllables (VT; AVT, EVT, IVT, OVT, UVT)

Examples: • *rain day all talk calm bald salt jaw wash wax quantity quack Paul caught*

• *see veil they eight ceiling key eider geyser height eat bread steak few Eugene*

• *pie piece mind sigh sign*

• *noise toy out group young bought rough plough dough growl show fool book shoal toe old yolk bolt doll poll cost most*

• *cue true suit*

Relevant (Distinctive) Features:

1. A vowel-team syllable has a cluster of two or three vowels or a vowel-consonant unit with a sound or sounds particular to that unit.

Irrelevant (Nondistinctive) Features:

1. The number of consonants before or after the cluster does not matter.

Many of these syllables have been called diphthong or digraph syllables. However, the labels *diphthong* and *digraph* do not clarify anything for the

IDENTIFYING MAGIC-E SYLLABLES (ALL VOWELS)

1.   **Put a 'vce' over every word that has one vowel, then one consonant, then an *e*.**

2.   **Arc under the magic-e syllables.**

Examples:
    vce take   vce Pete   vce tone   she   vce ate   vce slide

- -

nine   lake   woke   cake   ice   sat   slope

use   tame   rule   see   eke   same   shoe

choke   lane   ate   slide   peace   time   ace

slope   set   use   broke   drape   to   tame

chance   prune   while   ode   kite   tie   bone

tune   eke   piece   plate   stone   flute   pier

pike   ape   we   ace   cute   home   tone   while

pie   rope   uke   lane   ram   trade   glide

cheep   jute   make   do   whine   tree   time

phone   strafe   dredge   ape   spike   tame

see   plume   these   ice   made   in   rode

SORTING MAGIC-E AND OTHER MARKER-E SYLLABLES

The words below are magic-e syllables or marker-e syllables that are not magic-e syllables. Write them on the lines below the appropriate column headings. The first three have been done for you.

rake ✓ dance ✓ please ✓ Steve   ice   fudge   spume

graze   sconce   niece   cringe   slide   prune

shame   dunce   mauve   rose   flounce   quote

scribe   cruise   fence   ode   ease   change   flute

MAGIC-E	OTHER MARKER-E
rake	_dance_
	please

learner and, as noted in Chapter II, a number of vowel-consonant units are not usually included in these two categories. It seems easiest for most students to learn all of the vowel and vowel-consonant units having sounds particular to the unit if these units are grouped together under the single heading, "vowel team."

Exercise 3.6   Review the six worksheets, IDENTIFYING V̲-VOWEL TEAMS IN SYLLABLES, on pages 13–18. Do them again for practice if you have not become automatic at recognizing the vowel-teams.

Exercise 3.7   Complete the exercise sheet, SORTING CLOSED, MAGIC-E, AND VOWEL-TEAM SYLLABLES, on page 50. (Answers are on page 131.)

⊗ Vowel-R Syllables (VR)

The *r* following a vowel modifies the sound of the vowel. A traditional label for some of these units is "r-controlled"; however, the label "vowel-r" more clearly characterizes the visual structure of the syllable. Since the *r* follows the vowel in syllables that otherwise look like closed, magic-e, or vowel-team syllables, the vowel-r syllables are subclassified into three distinct types: vowel-r-closed syllables, vowel-r-magic-e syllables, and vowel-r-vowel-team syllables.

Note that the words ending in a marker-e that is <u>not</u> a magic-e (such as *large* and *pierce*) have the vowel sound that would be used if the *e* were not there. Thus, the words with a v̲r̲c̲e pattern have the same sounds that the vowel-r-closed syllables have, and the words with a v̲v̲r̲c̲e pattern have the same sound as the vowel-r-vowel-team syllables have.

⊗ Vowel-R-Closed (and Vowel-R-Closed + Marker-E) Syllables (VR-CL)

Examples: *car or warm word her urn shirt barge horse nurse*

Relevant (Distinctive) Features:

1. A vowel-r-closed syllable has one and only one vowel followed by an *r*.

or

2. It has one vowel followed by an *r*, another consonant, and a final *e*.

SORTING CLOSED, MAGIC-E, AND VOWEL-TEAM SYLLABLES

The syllables below are either closed, magic-e, or vowel-team syllables. Write them on the lines below the appropriate column headings. The first three have been done for you.

chrome ✓ toll ✓ Gwen ✓ sloe phlox lash use pie
these choice sigh lace free log imp lawn
next flute stun ode fray up chew spice
gift quake think old true pine rude oz
aught peace phlegm ate stand time tone

CLOSED	MAGIC-E	VOWEL-TEAM
Gwen	chrome	toll

Irrelevant (Nondistinctive) Features:

1. The particular vowel used does not matter.

2. The particular consonants used after the *r* or before the vowel do not matter.

3. The number of consonants appearing before the vowel or after the *r* does not matter.

Exercise 3.8   Review the worksheet, IDENTIFYING VOWEL-R-CLOSED UNITS IN SYLLABLES, on page 19. Do it again if you are not automatic at recognizing the vowel-r units.

Exercise 3.9   Complete the exercise sheet, SORTING VOWEL-R-CLOSED AND CLOSED SYLLABLES, on page 52. (Answers are on page 132.)

◈ Vowel-R-Magic-E Syllables (VR-ME)

Vowel-r-magic-e syllables are often taught along with regular magic-e syllables. For many learners, that seems to work just fine; for others, the difference in the sound of the vowel followed by *r* leads to confusion. It seems to be easier if these are kept separate from the other magic-e words.

As noted above, there are words containing a vowel-r unit that end in a marker *e* which is silent but does not mark the vowel; they are *not* VR-ME words. For example, *large* fits the VR-CL category in sound, as does *nurse*; *fierce* fits the VR-VT category, as we shall see below.

Examples: *care ire pure lore here -ore -ire -ure*

Relevant (Distinctive) Features:

1. A vowel-r-magic-e syllable ends in an *e*.

2. It has one and only one *r* before the ending *e*.

3. It has one and only one vowel before the *r*.

Irrelevant (Nondistinctive) Features:

1. The particular vowel used as the first vowel does not matter.

2. Except for the *r*, the particular consonants used do not matter.

3. The number of consonants before the vowel does not matter.

SORTING VOWEL-R-CLOSED AND CLOSED SYLLABLES

The words below are vowel-r-closed syllables or closed syllables. Write them on the lines below the appropriate column headings. The first three have been done for you.

car✓ trump✓ hurl✓ sham   herd   work   left   firm
shunt   perk   dwarf   stint   horse   chop   charm
chant   best   warp   rich   short   stretch   pant
bird   stump   nurse   flock

VOWEL-R-CLOSED

car

hurl

CLOSED

trump

◇ **Vowel-R-Vowel-Team Syllables (VR-VT)**

Examples: <u>air</u> <u>deer</u> <u>smear</u> <u>learn</u> <u>swear</u> <u>tour</u> <u>course</u> <u>hour</u> <u>door</u> <u>hoard</u>
<u>pierce</u>

Relevant (Distinctive) Features:

1. A vowel-r-vowel-team syllable is a cluster of two or three vowels followed by an *r*, having a sound or sounds particular to that unit.

Irrelevant (Nondistinctive) Features:

1. The particular consonants used before or after the unit do not matter.

2. The number of consonants before or after the unit does not matter.

Exercise 3.10 Review the worksheet, IDENTIFYING VOWEL-R VOWEL TEAMS IN SYLLABLES, on page 20.

Exercise 3.11 Complete the exercise sheet, SORTING VOWEL-R-CLOSED, VOWEL-R-MAGIC-E, AND VOWEL-R-VOWEL-TEAM SYLLABLES, on page 54. (Answers are on page 133.)

❖ **Consonant-L-E Syllables (<u>C</u>LE)**

The consonant-l-e syllables are:

ble, cle, dle, fle, gle, kle, ple, sle, tle, vle, zle

They never form words by themselves, and, except for words ending in the suffixes *-able* and *-ible*, they are almost always the second syllables of two-syllable words.

The vowel sound in the <u>C</u>LE syllables is the schwa sound (ə) that occurs before the *l*.[2] This is the same sound as is heard in the coarticulation of /ā/ and /l/ (*bale*) or /ē/ and /l/ (*seal*). The unaccented vowel sound that is automatically attached to most consonants when they are pronounced in isolation may be represented by the ə. Thus, *l* (by itself) is pronounced either as /əl/ or as /lə/. At the end of a <u>C</u>LE syllable, the glide from the previous (consonant) sound to the *l* provides the vowel sound for that syllable, making the pronunciation /əl/ (as in /tā/′/bəl/). This vowel sound is denoted in

---

[2]The schwa sound is described in Chapter I (on page 5). It is also discussed at the beginning of Chapter IV (on page 64).

SORTING VOWEL-R-CLOSED, VOWEL-R-MAGIC-E, AND VOWEL-R-VOWEL-TEAM SYLLABLES

The words below are VR-CL, VR-ME, or VR-VT syllables. Write them on the lines below the appropriate column headings. Remember that a marker-e does not affect the vowel, so a VR-VT syllable with a marker-e at the end goes with VR-VT, and a VR-CL syllable with a marker-e goes with VR-CL. The first three have been done for you.

cart✓ dire✓ air✓ Thor   hear   tier   care   germ
Moore   lyre   clear   coarse   wore   fare   stir
flair   warm   shire   quart   terse   fierce   score
urge   hour   sphere   birch   pure   word   queer
here   square   rear   horde

VR-CLOSED	**VR-MAGIC-E**	**VR-VOWEL-TEAM**
cart	*dire*	*air*

dictionaries either as c̲'l (ta·b'l) or as c̲əl (ta·bəl). Since there is no *other* vowel sound in a C̲LE syllable, the ending *e* just marks the syllable visually.

Most of these words are Anglo-Saxon in origin, consisting of a base word and the suffix *-le*. When pronouncing and decoding words, it is often the case that we break a word into syllables at a spot other than at the division between the base and the affix. The consonant-l-e words provide clear examples of this. We do not say /nōb/·/əl/; rather, we say /nō/·/bəl/. The pronunciation pattern for these words is extremely regular, *provided that* the consonant before the *le* is kept as part of the last syllable—the syllable preceding the *-c̲le* is pronounced as if the *-c̲le* were not there.

Examples: *table   marble   fizzle   noble   bugle   puddle   simple   title   needle*
  bauble   purple   circle   wrestle

Relevant (Distinctive) Features:

1. The name of this syllable type describes its distinctive feature—it is a consonant followed by *le*.

Irrelevant (Nondistinctive) Features:

1. The particular consonant appearing before the *l* does not matter.

Exercise 3.12   Complete the worksheet, IDENTIFYING CONSONANT-L-E SYLLABLES, on page 56.

❈ Sound Patterns in Monosyllabic Words ❈

In monosyllabic words, the vowel sounds for the syllable types are quite regular:

- Closed syllables have short vowel sounds.
- Magic-e and open syllables have long vowel sounds.
- Vowel-team syllables and vowel-r syllables have sounds that are specific to the particular vowel-team or vowel-r unit.

(The C̲LE syllables never occur in monosyllabic words.)

There is a relatively small set of words that do not follow the regular sound patterns. They are often called **irregular words** or **outlaw words**.

IDENTIFYING CONSONANT-L-E SYLLABLES

Arc under the cle syllable in each word.

Examples: sample   idle   rattle   gargle   noble

- -

nimble   toggle   example   huddle   feeble

purple   double   gentle   ramble   miracle

fiddle   snuggle   hurdle   bauble   rifle

stumble   steeple   waddle   circle   poodle

scruple   straggle   throttle   Myrtle   rumble

beagle   cradle   whistle   rustle   turtle

staple   jiggle   barnacle   rumple   hobble

paddle   stifle   needle   startle   ogle handle

trestle   bugle   warble   waffle   goggle

truffle   fizzle   temple   trouble   table

sidle   crackle   tingle   purple   measle

rattle   uncle   able   eagle   muscle   title

(The label "outlaw" seems to help children remember that these words don't "follow the rules"; that is, the sounds in these words don't fit the usual patterns.) Although the number of irregular words is quite small in comparison to the regular ones, many of the irregular words are among the most commonly used words in our language, making the task of beginning to read even harder for children who have memory difficulties.

Here are some examples of common irregular words:

- *the, to, do, who* — These should have long vowel sounds because they are open syllables (like *me* and *go*).

- *what, was, whom* — These should have short vowel sounds because they are closed syllables (like *sat* and *cot*).

- *again, against, says, said* — These should have long *a* sounds because of the *ai* vowel team (like *say* and *pain*).

- *been* — This should have a long *e* sound (like *seen*).

There are also a number of words in which the *o* says /ŭ/, instead of /ŏ/ or /ō/; for example:

of   from   son   month   front   some   love   other   money   among

(This deviation is so common that I teach my students to try /ŭ/ when the "correct" sound for *o* doesn't work.)

One of the teaching materials available as an accompaniment to this book is a list of most of the monosyllabic English words, sorted according to syllable structures and vowel sounds.[3] Nearly all of the irregular monosyllabic words are included in this list.

Exercise 3.13   Complete the following worksheets. Then say the sound for the vowel grapheme in each word. Finally, read the words aloud and listen for the vowel sounds as you read.

  (a) MARKING THE SHORT AND LONG VOWEL SOUNDS IN CLOSED AND MAGIC-E SYLLABLES, on page 59;

  (b) MARKING THE VOWELS IN A-VOWEL-TEAM SYLLABLES, on pages 60 and 61;

  (c) MARKING THE VOWELS IN VOWEL-R-CLOSED SYLLABLES, on page 62.

---

[3] Contact Oxton House, Publishers, for further information about this list and other auxiliary materials.

Exercise 3.14   Be sure that you know the diacritical marks and sounds for the vowel teams. Use the vowel-team pictures (on pages 104–109) to help yourself memorize them. Read the words on the six worksheets IDENTIFYING <u>V</u>-VOWEL-TEAMS IN SYLLABLES (on pages 13–18) and the worksheet IDENTIFY-ING VOWEL-R VOWEL-TEAMS IN SYLLABLES (on page 20), listening for the sounds of the vowel graphemes as you read.

MARKING THE VOWELS IN CLOSED AND MAGIC-E SYLLABLES

1. If the word is a closed syllable, mark the vowel short.

2. If the word is a magic-e syllable, mark the vowel long.

Examples: tāke hŭnt clăsp sōle īce sĕt

- -

nine hop wish lake us tone clash

flute rest rule eke egg same step at

choke lane pat ate trump time ace

slop set use broke drape loft tame

class prune whip odd kite tint bone

left stretch eke trust plate stone

flute punt pick wrench ace cute home

ship while plank rob uke clone trap

glide chip jute ice mask dock whine

ump these grump inch clash up twelfth

rhyme eve romp tile such stretch ice

MARKING THE VOWELS IN A-VOWEL-TEAM SYLLABLES

Put the diacritical mark above each a-vowel team.

Examples: m̄ain   m̂aul   st̂all   ĉalm   b̂ald

- -

chain   all   Paul   calm   scald   balm   haul

drain   ball   pail   bald   fault   tall

ribald   palm   traipse   alms   sprain   all

small   scald   cause   psalm   aim   fraud

aid   fall   bald   train   gauze   becalm

maul   faint   call   haunt   scald   paint

pause   mall   calmly   bald   sail   sauce

stall   fail   ribald   balm   vault   ball

main   calm   launch   palm   small   bald

braid   hall   balm   jail   caulk   mauve

scald   braille   calm   staunch   stall

MARKING THE VOWELS IN A-VOWEL-TEAM SYLLABLES

Put the diacritical mark above each a-vowel team.

Examples: pāy   drâw   câught   sâlt   wâlk

- -

say   saw   malt   aught   talk   caught

bay   asphalt   chalk   shawl   salt   may

clay   flaw   taught   talk   spray   stalk

naughty   halt   draw   stray   daughter

awning   salt   ray   emerald   naught   gray

Balkan   law   cobalt   day   chalk   caught

malt   dawn   Kay   talk   spawn   pay   fraught

play   Falkland   slay   exalt   yawn   haughty

drawn   tray   lay   taught   balk   asphalt

day   stalk   paw   halt   caught   malt   fray

spawn   stray   fraught   salt   aye   chalk

MARKING THE VOWELS IN VOWEL-R-CLOSED SYLLABLES

Put the proper diacritical mark above each vr or wvr unit.

Examples: bärn   cu̇rl   her̈   dir̈t   fôr   wâr   wȯrk

- -

car   skirt   worth   sort   large   blurb   herd

work   arm   warm   yard   sir   dwarf   Herb

morn   hurl   worse   harm   term   ward   swirl

warp   start   burst   cork   starve   worst

work   bird   her   horse   worst   harsh   twerp

short   urge   world   fork   part   thwart

burst   curl   warm   perk   dwarf   ward   first

curb   torque   word   firm   war   charm   slur

her   twirl   merge   York   fur   worst   jar

fern   force   urn   worth   bird   warm   yarn

perk   dwarf   charge   short   harsh   warn

IV

Multisyllable Words

The majority of English words have more than one syllable. Most of these multisyllable words are made up of a root and affixes, though some are just root words and some are compound words. In order to decode multisyllable words, one must recognize the number of syllables in a word. One must also recognize affixes, be able to divide the word into syllables according to syllable division patterns, and identify the individual words in a compound word. Additionally, to pronounce the vowel sounds correctly, one must know how the accent patterns affect the vowel sound patterns of multisyllable words. Dividing a word into its syllables according to the syllable division patterns and recognizing the affixes will often help to determine the accent or stress pattern. Since these are skills that poor readers acquire only with difficulty and assistance, it is important that they be taught systematically and carefully.

The accent, or stress pattern, of a multisyllable word determines to a large degree the vowel sound given to each syllable. In English, we typically accent two- and three-syllable words on the first syllable. When a syllable is accented or stressed, it usually retains the vowel sound that it would have in a monosyllabic word. Thus, in the word *tandem*, the first syllable is accented. As a monosyllable, *tan* has a short vowel sound (/ă/), and it has the same sound in this multisyllable word; the syllable is pronounced just as though you were saying the monosyllabic word *tan*. The second syllable, however, is unaccented and therefore does not sound the same as it would if it were a monosyllabic word *dem* (which would rhyme with *them*). Instead, its vowel sound is glossed over, not pronounced as clearly as it is in a monosyllabic word. Think about the word *signal*. The first syllable, *sig*, is pronounced just as though it were a monosyllabic word. The second (unaccented) syllable, *nal*, does not sound the same as it would if it were accented. If accented, it would have a short *a* sound and would rhyme with *pal*. Instead, it has an indistinct sound, a glossed-over sound that makes it seem almost as though it is part of the *l* that follows it. This glossed-over vowel sound of unaccented syllables is the schwa sound, which was introduced in Chapter I.

All single vowels, vowel teams, and vowel-r units can have the schwa sound when they appear in an unaccented syllable, and the schwa sound is pretty much the same no matter how it is spelled. For all single vowels and vowel teams, the schwa sound ranges from a clear /ŭ/ sound to a sound that is close to /ĭ/; but it is clearly a glossed-over sound in an unstressed syllable when a word is pronounced at its normal speed. When the schwa vowel is followed by a consonant in the same syllable, it seems almost as though it is part of that consonant sound. For practice in hearing this, say the following words as you normally would in a sentence, listening for the sound you hear for the underlined vowel:

| *happen* | *mental* | *wisdom* | *fossil* | *portrait* |
| *circuit* | *accuse* | *compete* | *irrigate* | *execute* |

For practice in hearing the schwa sound for vowel-r units, say these words as you normally would in a sentence:

| *better* | *supper* | *doctor* | *color* | *actor* | *dollar* |
| *alligator* | *advisor* | *burglar* | *calendar* | *caterpillar* |

Dictionaries use words such as 'neutral,' 'indistinct,' 'uncolored,' and 'indeterminate' to describe the schwa sound. 'Indeterminate' captures the sense that the sound is not determined by the vowel used to spell the word. Think of the difficulty you would have in knowing how to spell a word containing the schwa sound if you had not learned its traditional spelling pattern (e.g., *acquaintance* vs. *independence*; *open* vs. *common*). The pronunciation of the schwa sound does not determine which vowel to use. People who are good spellers have a hard time understanding how one could not just know which vowel to use; people who are poor spellers have a hard time understanding how in the world you can possibly know which vowel to use for those indeterminate schwa sounds!

Perhaps by this time you are objecting loudly that you never did "get" accenting. If that is the case, it's OK. Many people have difficulty focusing on the stress patterns as they pronounce words. Hearing the vowel sound in the unstressed syllable is even more difficult because when you focus on that vowel you tend to pronounce it more clearly and stress it more than you do when you are not focusing on it. Also, people use different dialects that affect the pronunciation of the unaccented syllables as well as of the accented syllables. When teaching decoding of multisyllable words, words are grouped according to their syllable structures, stress patterns, and vowel sounds, so that students gradually get better at distinguishing the stress patterns in these words. The general principle to remember is that any single vowel, vowel-r unit, or vowel team, whether in the stem or an affix, usually (but not always) has the schwa sound if it occurs in an unstressed syllable.

A rendition of the specific skills needed to decode the many different multisyllable word structures would result in a very long list. Although the sequence in which these skills are taught is not particularly important, adding suffixes to one-syllable words should precede adding suffixes to multisyllable words, and teaching syllable division patterns using two-syllable words should precede similar work on words of more than two syllables. In the following descriptions of the multisyllable word patterns, suffix patterns are presented first because suffixes appear with regularity in beginning reading material.

⊰⊱ Prefixes and Suffixes ⊰⊱

affix (ə fiks′) [*verb, transitive*] to fasten or attach (something to something else).

affix (af′iks) [*noun*] something that is attached or joined to something else; esp., a word part, consisting of one or more syllables, that is attached to a root word or word stem in order to modify or change the meaning.

prefix [*noun*] an affix attached to the beginning of a word or word stem.

suffix [*noun*] an affix attached to the end of a word or word stem.

Most multisyllable words in our language are made up of a **root** (also called a **base** or a **stem**), which may or may not be used as a word in English, and one or more prefixes and/or suffixes. (See Appendix B for a comprehensive list of common prefixes and suffixes.)

Prefixes will not be discussed in detail because they are usually added to words or roots without changing the spelling of the word or root. The root typically is or contains the accented syllable, and most Latin roots are easily decoded. Additionally, when we add a prefix to a commonly used word, the pronunciation of the root word seldom changes (e.g., *unlike, uneasy, refit, replay, imperfect*). Prefixes are commonly added to roots that are not used as words in English. For example:

$$pre + dict = predict \qquad re + buke = rebuke \qquad ad + tain = attain$$

Often the spelling of the prefix is changed to make pronunciation easier; however, when learning to decode these words, we usually treat them as ordinary multisyllable words that follow the regular syllable division patterns. Direct instruction on the meanings of affixes and root words is extremely beneficial for reading comprehension *after* readers have learned to decode the words. Thus, pursuit of that interesting topic lies beyond the scope of this book.

Prefixes and suffixes usually add syllables to a word, but there are a few suffixes that do not add a syllable. They are part of the group that are often called the "easy endings." The "easy-ending" suffixes are:

$$-s \qquad -es \qquad -\text{'}s \qquad -ed \qquad -ing \qquad -er \qquad -est \qquad -y \qquad -ly$$

(I have not found the origin of the label "easy ending" and, given the difficulty with which many poor readers learn these suffixes, it may be a misnomer.) The *-s* and *-'s* suffixes do not add a syllable to a word unless the word ends in one of the sounds /s/, /ch/, /sh/, or /z/, in which case *-es* replaces *s* (*cats, Pam's*, but *dresses*). The suffix *-ed* adds a syllable as a visual structure, and adds an auditory syllable when it is pronounced as /əd/ (*handed*), but not when it is pronounced as /d/ or /t/ (*slammed, pounced*). The rest of the suffixes add both a visual and auditory syllable. The easy-ending suffixes usually are taught very early because it is difficult to write stories without them.

In the following descriptions of the rules by which we add suffixes to words, the majority of the examples contain easy-ending suffixes. All suffixes are added to words using the same spelling rules; thus, once the rules for reading and spelling words with the easy-ending suffixes have been taught, proper usage of the rest of the suffixes generally follows directly from the mastery of their meanings and pronunciations. The rules for adding suffixes to words are used more obviously when spelling than when reading. Remember, however, that it is the spelling patterns that we look at when we read, so the changes in a root word that result from adding a suffix dictate how the word is to be pronounced. When teaching emerging readers to read these words, we teach them to identify the suffix as a visual unit, then to identify the root word (by identifying its syllable structure and, therefore, its vowel sound), and finally to decode the whole word. Once the recognition of the root word with the added suffix becomes fluent, the reader does not need to focus on these steps separately.

⊗⊗ Rules for Adding Suffixes ⊗⊗

⊗ The Doubling (or 1-1-1) Rule

> For one-syllable base words (or compounds of one-syllable words), if the base word ends in only one consonant and has only one vowel before it, and if the suffix begins with a vowel, then the consonant ending the base word is doubled.

If you think about the syllable types, you will realize that this rule applies to adding suffixes to closed syllables and to vowel-r-closed syllables.

Examples of doubling:

can̲n̲ing	*bat̲t̲er*	*fun̲n̲y*	*hot̲t̲est*	*step̲p̲ed*	*hug̲g̲able*
red̲d̲ish	*mar̲r̲ed*	*stir̲r̲er*	*whir̲r̲ing*	*war̲r̲ior*	*blur̲r̲y*

The consonant ending the base word is not doubled if the suffix begins with a consonant, if there is more than one consonant at the end of the base word, or if there is more than one vowel in the base word.

Examples of no doubling:

can̲s	*sin̲ful*	*sad̲ly*	*top̲less*	*scar̲less*	*pac̲king*
stum̲ped	*har̲sher*	*stor̲my*	*ra̲iny*	*gro̲wing*	

The convenience of teaching this as the "1-1-1 Rule" is that, if you have the students put 'v' or 'c' above the letters starting with the first vowel in the base word and continuing through the first letter of the suffix, and if they have one vowel, one consonant, and another vowel, then they know that they need to double the consonant. Remembering "1-1-1" is an easy mnemonic for the verbal rule.

For a reader, this means that a single vowel in a word with two consonants before the suffix will be short, unless the consonants create a vowel team (which the students will have to memorize) or unless the consonants are *r*'s. Words with a <u>*vrrv*</u> pattern are a bit harder to read until they become sight words.

Words such as *star* and *blur* become *starry* and *blurring*, for example, when a suffix beginning with a vowel is added, and they are pronounced in the expected way—as a VR-CL syllable plus the suffix. However, there are a number of words that look like these (*carry, marry, berry*) but are not base words plus suffixes, and their vowel sounds are not those of VR-CL syllables. (See the notes on vowels before *r*, on page 82 in the section on pronunciation of multisyllable words.)

As usual, there are some oddities or irregularities to our language. One that needs attention while working on the doubling rule with one-syllable words is the handling of *x*. Remember that *x* has the sound /ks/ at the end of words. If you think of it as two letters (my students draw a line down the middle of it— ⅹ —and write k|s above it, if necessary), you can apply the doubling rule. If you think of it as one letter, it is an exception to the rule because you do not double it when adding suffixes (*taxing, waxy, mixer, fixable*).

> For multisyllable words, the doubling rule is the same (1-1-1), but applies *only when* the last syllable of the root is accented (which is not the most common accent pattern).

Examples of doubling:

be·gin′<u>ner</u>	al·lot′<u>ted</u>	ad·mit′<u>tance</u>	re·fit′<u>ting</u>
ab·hor′<u>red</u>	con·cur′<u>ring</u>	de·ter′<u>rent</u>	oc·cur′<u>rence</u>

Examples of no doubling:

Suffix begins with a consonant: *forgetful*   *allot<u>ment</u>*

admit<u>s</u>   begin<u>s</u>   refit<u>s</u>   abhor<u>s</u>   deter<u>ment</u>

Last syllable of root not accented: *ran′somed   fas′tener*

blos′soming   can′celable   cus′tomize   ben′e·fited

Of course, there are words that don't follow the rule. Some words change accent pattern as suffixes are added. In some of these cases, it seems that the words follow the accent pattern before the suffix is added; in others, it seems that the spelling pattern is what you would expect after the accent change. For example, the verb *prefer* is stressed on the second syllable, and the *r* is indeed doubled when adding *-ed*, *-ing*, and *-er* (*preferred, preferring, preferrer*); when *-able* and *-ence* are added, the stress changes to the first syllable and there is only one *r*, as one would expect when the last syllable is unaccented (*pref′erable, pref′erence*). The words *prefer, defer, confer*, and *refer* all work this way.

Infer works the same way except when adding *-able*; since *inferable* has only one *r*, you would *not* expect *fer* to be accented, but it is. (From the spelling side, since *inferable* is accented on the *fer*, you would expect two *r*'s, but use only one.)

Transfer is even messier; the accent shifts from the first to the second syllable, and alternate spellings are acceptable. (As you study this word, think about which accent pattern you usually use for its different forms.) *Trans·fer′ring, trans·fer′red*, and *trans·fer′rer* have the expected double *r*'s, but *trans·fer′able* and *trans·fer′al* are listed first in dictionaries, with *trans·fer′rable* and *trans·fer′ral* as alternate spellings. Moreover, *transference* is listed with *trans·fer′ence* and *trans′fer·ence* as alternate pronunciations; but the first of these pronunciations creates a spelling irregularity, since two *r*'s would normally be expected. Table 2 may help you visualize the pattern for these words.

Words that end in *l* can also be confusing. The British spelling pattern doubles the *l* when adding suffixes, even if the syllable is unaccented; the American pattern follows the accent pattern and does not double the *l* if the syllable is not accented. Thus, the *l* in *travel* would be doubled for *travelling* in British spelling, but not in American (*traveling*). The doubled *l* is listed as an acceptable but less preferred spelling in the American dictionaries. Some of you may automatically double the *l* in some words (e.g., *counselling*), especially if you have been taught spelling by someone who follows the British pattern, or if you have lived in a country strongly influenced by British schooling. Since always doubling the *l* adds another complexity to the pattern, in the United States it is better to include these words when teaching the regular pattern.

Exercise 4.1   Complete the exercise sheet, USING THE DOUBLING RULE TO ADD SUFFIXES, on page 70. (Answers are on page 134.)

USING THE DOUBLING RULE TO ADD SUFFIXES

Add the given suffixes to the following words. If you did not double the ending consonant, indicate why not.   Three of them have been done for you.

can + ing

canning

fish + es
cc

fishes

step + ed

_____

tax + ing

_____

jump + y

_____

nut + y

_____

tax + able

_____

dim + est

_____

sad + ly

_____

war + s

_____

storm + y

_____

harm + less

_____

star + y

_____

tar + ed

_____

firm + ly

_____

stir + able

_____

spur + ed

_____

market + ing

marketing

control + ed

_____

forget + able

_____

sudden + ly

_____

transmit + ed

_____

allot + ment

_____

complex + ity

_____

master + ing

_____

admit + ance

_____

pilot + ed

_____

Root word	Last syllable of root accented—consonant doubled	First syllable accented—consonant not doubled
prefer	*preferring, preferred*	*preference, preferable*
defer	*deferring, deferred, deferral*	*deference*
confer	*conferring, conferred, conferral*	*conference, conferee*
refer	*referring, referred, referral*	*reference, referee*
infer	*inferring, inferred, inferrer* *inferable* is irregular	*inference*
transfer	*transferring, transferred* *transferrer* *transferable* and *transferal* are irregular, but their alternate spellings are regular: *transferrable, transferral* *transference* is irregular, but ...	*transferee, transferase* *transference* is regular

The *-fer* words.

Table 2

❖ The Silent-E Rule

> For both monosyllabic and multisyllable words, when a word ends in a silent *e* and the suffix begins with a vowel, we almost always drop the *e* before adding the suffix.

This rule applies to magic-e syllables, vowel-r-magic-e syllables, the marker-e words of all syllable types (with one variation), and cLE syllables (with one variation). The vowel-team syllables ending in *e* (*ue, i(y)e, oe,* and *ee*) are a bit messy.

Examples of dropping the *e*:

> *taking   nicer   wisest   mulish   wired   purest   bony   fizzled*
>
> *rattling   desirous   creativity   disposing   concretize*

One of the confusions (but *not* irregularities) with this rule is created by the words that end in *-ey* when the *y* is not a suffix (e.g., *Coney* (Island), *Smiley, Casey*). Name-words of this kind are quite common and often overlap with common words in which the *y* *is* a suffix (e.g., *Smokey, smoky*; *Lacey, lacy*). In addition, there are a few words listed twice as separate entries in dictionaries, with the *-ey* entry referring to the *-y* entry, (e.g., *nosey, nosy*), and a few with both spellings listed together. In the majority of cases, however, the *e* in a magic-e syllable is dropped before adding the suffix *-y*.

Do not drop a silent *e* if the suffix begins with a consonant.

Examples:

> wise*ly*   state*me*nt   care*f*ul   home*le*ss   tire*so*me
>
> concrete*ly*   displace*me*nt   complete*ne*ss   involve*me*nt

There is a variation that applies to marker-e words. Sometimes the silent *e* marks something besides the vowel in the base word, and this *e* must be kept to preserve what it marks. For example, since the suffix *-able* begins with a vowel, a silent *e* in the base word is usually dropped (*framable, definable*). However, the letters *c* and *g* in words such as *race* and *singe* would change from their soft sounds to their hard sounds if the *e* were dropped (*racable, singable*), so it is not dropped in these cases (*raceable, singeable*). This pattern is relatively common (*courageous, vengeance, manageable*, etc.) and needs to be learned as a concept.

The variation for CLE syllables occurs when using *-ly* to form an adjective or adverb. For most words, we just add the *-ly* and pronounce the words with an extra syllable (*sadly, wisely, finally, aerially, courageously*). When changing the form of these CLE words, however, instead of *adding* the suffix *-ly*, we change the suffix *-le* to *-ly*; the pronunciation of this final syllable thereby changes from /cəl/ to /clē/ (*wobble* to *wobbly, nimble* to *nimbly*). This same change occurs when we make adverbs out of words ending in the suffixes *-able* and *-ible* (*comfortable* to *comfortably, incredible* to *incredibly*). For decoding, the words follow the same pattern as when they end in CLE (see page 78). For spelling, even though it seems that the easiest way to deal with adding *-ly* to CLE words is just to change the *e* to *y*, I like to tell my students to change the *le* to *ly*, thereby preserving the suffix as a meaningful unit. For the rest of the suffixes, the CLE syllables follow the rule for dropping the silent *e* (*rifles, babbled, bubbling, ambler, gentlest*).

The problem with the vowel-team words that end in *e* occurs when adding the suffix *-ing*:

- When the word ends in *ee* or *oe*, just add the *-ing*: *seeing, agreeing, toeing, hoeing, canoeing*, etc.

- When the word ends in *ue*, drop the *e*: *cuing, bluing, ruing, suing, cluing, gluing*. Although half of these have alternate spellings (*cueing, blueing, trueing*), it is best to teach them all alike.

- When the word ends in *ye*, keep the *e*: *dyeing, eyeing*. But when the word ends in *ie*, change the *ie* to *y*: *dying* (as opposed to 'living'), *lying, tying, vying*. The verb *die* that means "to mold, stamp, or cut" is an exception; its *-ing* form is *dieing*.

And then there are some common oddities or irregularities:

- *duly, truly*, and *wholly* drop the *e* before the *-ly*;

- *awful* drops the *e* before *-ful*; *argument* drops the *e* before *-ment*;

- alternate spellings of *abridgment* and *acknowledgment* retain the *e*, thereby keeping the soft sound of the *g* apparent;

- *judgement* is a less preferred spelling of *judgment*, though it is the accepted British spelling.

- *mileage* and *acreage* keep the *e* before a vowel for no apparent reason.

Exercise 4.2   Complete the exercise sheet, USING THE SILENT-E RULE TO ADD SUFFIXES, on page 74. (Answers are on page 135.)

❈ Adding Suffixes to Words That End in Y

> For words that end in *y*, if there is a vowel before the *y*, just add the suffix, regardless of whether the suffix begins with a vowel or consonant.

In terms of syllable types, it is the vowel-team syllables that end in *y* (*ay, ey, oy*) that fit this pattern. This pattern is also used with the two open syllable words that have a silent *u* before the *y* (*buy* and *guy*). Since there are relatively few words that end in one of these vowel teams, there will not be many words that follow this pattern.

USING THE SILENT-E RULE TO ADD SUFFIXES

Add the given suffixes to the following words. If you did not drop the e, indicate why not. Two of them have been done for you.

bike + s̆ᶜ

__bikes_____

square + er

_____

dribble + ing

_____

cute + est

__cutest_____

large + ly

_____

village + s

_____

scheme + ed

_____

ice + y

_____

compete + ing

_____

time + ly

_____

crackle + y

_____

capsize + ed

_____

care + ful

_____

singe + ing

_____

festive + ity

_____

skate + ing

_____

serve + er

_____

purple + ish

_____

size + able

_____

insane + ly

_____

handle + ed

_____

dance + ing

_____

accuse + atory

_____

excite + ment

_____

pure + est

_____

active + ate

_____

change + able

_____

Examples:

> *plays   obeyed   payable   coyness   employment   buying*

Irregulars:

> *laid   paid   said   slain   daily   gaily*

> For words that end in *y*, if there is a consonant before the *y*,
> we usually change the *y* to *i* before adding any suffix except
> *-ing* and *-ish*.

This pattern is common when the suffix *-y* has been added to a root and
then another suffix is added on to that (*nose, nosy, nosiness*). It can be
difficult for many students.

Examples:

> *angrily   merriment   warily   laziness   tiniest*
>
> *holier   candied   ladies*

Since we don't use two *i*'s together in English words, the *y* is *not* changed
to *i* before adding *-ing* or *-ish*.

Examples:

> *babying   babyish   signifying   applying   worrying*
>
> *denying   verifying*

One common exception is *ski*, which ends in *i* and is borrowed, unmodified,
from Norwegian; thus, *skiing*.

The monosyllabic, open-syllable words that end in *y* (*shy, wry, fly, ply,
sly*, etc.) are not nearly as regular as one would wish. Thankfully, these words
don't combine with very many suffixes. The *y* does not change before *-ing*,
nor does it change before *-ly* or *-ness*, the only consonant-beginning suffixes
that these take: *drying, prying,* ...; *shyly, shyness, wryly, wryness, slyly,
slyness, dryly, dryness, spryly, spryness*. Some of the words are consistent in
changing the *y* to *i* before the rest of the suffixes:

> *wry: wrier, wriest*
>
> *ply: plied, plier, pliers, plies*
>
> *cry: cried, crier, cries*

> *pry:* *pried, pries, prier*
> *try:* *tried, trier, tries, trial, triable*
> *spy:* *spier* (alt. for the noun *spy*), *spied, spies*

Some of the words are not consistent or have both spellings listed. Alternate spellings are listed here in the order in which they are found in most dictionaries, with a notation if one spelling goes with a particular meaning, or if one spelling is preferred (as opposed to being just an alternate).

> *shy:* *shier* (noun), as a horse that shies; *shied, shies*;
> *shyer, shier*; and *shyest, shiest* (adj.)
>
> *sly:* *slyer, slier*; *slyest, sliest*
>
> *fly:* *flies*; *flyable*; *flier, flyer* (more common when talking
> about a train, plane, or bus, or an aviator)
>
> *dry:* *dried*; *driest*; *dries*; *dryable*;
> *drier* as an additive to paint, etc.;
> *dryer* as a person, machine, rack, etc.
>
> *fry:* *fried*; *fries*; *fryer* preferred, as in young chicken,
> machine, etc., *frier*
>
> *spry:* *sprier, spryer*; *spriest, spryest*

To put it simply, you could teach your students to change the *y* to *i* except when talking about (1) a person or machine that dries or flies, or something that is dryable or flyable, and (2) something that can be fried, or the person or machine that does the frying. This just takes lots of practice.

Exercise 4.3   Complete the exercise sheet, ADDING SUFFIXES TO WORDS ENDING IN Y, on page 77. (Answers are on page 136.)

⬖⬖⬖ Compound Words ⬖⬖⬖

A **compound word** is a word made up of two or more words that are spelled normally and, for the most part, retain their usual meanings. Compound words often are the first set of multisyllable words taught because (1) it is easy to recognize the short, known words within these words, and (2) each of the short words is accented, so there are no accent or stress patterns (and resulting schwa vowel sounds) to confuse the reader.

ADDING SUFFIXES TO WORDS ENDING IN *Y*

Add the given suffixes to the following words. If you did not
change the *y* to *i* before adding the suffix, indicate why not.
Two of them have been done for you.

try + ed **tried**	lazy + er _____	coy + ly _____
pry + es _____	lazy + ly _____	spy + es _____
ꞓ y + i pry + ing **prying**	gray + er _____	comply + ing _____
dry + ly _____	pacify + ing _____	heavy + est _____
play + ful _____	lazy + ness _____	family + ar _____
envy + able _____	lucky + ly _____	factory + es _____
silly + est _____	weary + er _____	fury + ous _____
decry + ing _____	sleepy + ish _____	marry + age _____
angry + est _____	library + an _____	defray + ed _____

Examples:

> *backpack   knapsack   mouthwash   sunlight   raindrop*
> *groundhog   handclasp   ragbag   afternoon   motorcar*

Exercise 4.4   From a page in a book or magazine, find and underline all compound words.

◈◈◈ Syllable Division Patterns ◈◈◈

In order to decode a multisyllable word that is neither a one-syllable root plus an affix nor a compound word, one must know how to divide the word into its syllables. In English, we use three basic syllable division patterns. The c̲le pattern is introduced first because it is the easiest to learn and because words containing the c̲le syllables are the most consistent in obeying the vowel sound rules.

◈ The c̲le Pattern

Most words containing consonant-le syllables are two-syllable words. To decode these words, keep the *cle* together as one syllable, dividing just before the *c̲*:

> *can·dle   ta·ble   ti·tle   rub·ble   gar·gle*
> *pur·ple   chor·tle   stee·ple   bau·ble*

The first syllable is the accented one, and it will have the sound that it normally has in a monosyllable. Therefore, the first syllables of the words just listed are pronounced like this:

$$/\text{can}/, /\text{tā}/, /\text{tĭ}/, /\text{rub}/, /\text{gar}/, /\text{pur}/, /\text{chor}/, /\text{stee}/, /\text{bau}/$$

There are close to 400 two-syllable words ending in a *cle* syllable, and only a few of them are truly irregular. (For instance, in *aisle* the *ai* says /ī/ instead of /ā/ and the *s* is silent; in *treble* the first *e* is short when it should be long; in *people* we use *eo* as a vowel team when it is usually split into two separate syllables.) There are a few other *regular* patterns that need to be practiced:

- When the first syllable ends in *s* and is followed by *tle*, the *t* is silent (*whistle, thistle, castle*).

- When the first syllable ends in *n* and is followed by *gle* or *kle*, the *n* is nasal, as in *ng* and *nk* (*jungle, strangle, ankle, twinkle*).

- In *axle*, the short sound of the *a* can be explained by treating the *x* as *ks* (*ak·sle*).

Several of the four dozen or so CLE words that have three or more syllables are compound words (*manhandle, sidesaddle*) or are two-syllable words with an added prefix (*recycle, rekindle*). Of the rest, some are accented on the syllable just before the *cle*, and that accented syllable has its normal vowel sound (such as /ăm/ in *ex·am·ple*, /sī/ in *dis·ci·ple*, and /pŏs/ in *a·pos·tle*. When the first syllable is accented, it has its normal vowel sound and the syllable just before the *cle* has the (unaccented) schwa sound (such as /nə/ in *bar·na·cle*, /nə/ in *mo·no·cle*, and /tə/ in *ar·ti·cle*).

The words containing the commonly used suffixes *-able* and *-ible* have to be decoded using the rules for suffixes and the next two syllable division rules, as appropriate.

There are a few words ending in a consonant plus *-re* that are decoded like the *cle* words:

> acre   massacre   mediocre   ogre   euchre
>
> timbre   cadastre   nacre   involucre

The problem with teaching these words as a pattern is that we use as many French and Spanish words ending in *cre* for which we retain the French or Spanish pronunciation:

> hombre   Andre   cadre   padre   emigre
>
> genre   entendre   d'etre   entre

Thus, it seems best to teach the *cre* words as they occur in reading material.

◈ The VCCV Pattern

Usually, when there are two or more consonants between the vowel units, the word is divided into syllables between the consonants, as in *pup·pet, men·tal, sym·bol, sup·pose,* and *doc·tor*. This is called the VCCV pattern. Underlining the vowel units and dividing the word into syllables allows the reader to determine the most probable vowel sound of the syllables. (Shifting the stress from one syllable to the other often changes the vowel sound, as in shifting between the noun and verb forms of words such as *ad'dress* [*ad·dress'*].)

When there are three consonants between the vowel units, two of them will be a single-sound consonant team or a consonant blend. These stay together when pronouncing the word; most readers become so fluent at recognizing these units that they do not try to divide them (e.g., in *fulcrum* we would automatically keep the *cr* together). When there is a doubled consonant and a different consonant, the word most often is divided between the two consonants that are the same (*mat·tress, at·tract*).

When the first syllable contains a vowel-r unit (*pardon, surplus, organ, harvest*), the syllable division usually is obvious—the *r*, of course, stays with the vowel, and consonant teams and blends tend to go in the second syllable (*sur·plus, ur·chin, or·phan*). When the first of two consonants following the *r* stays in the first syllable, it is usually because this consonant does not join with the next one in a SSCT or a blend. For example, as in *arc·tic*, *ct* cannot occur as a blend at the beginning of a syllable. (A fuller discussion of vowel-r graphemes in multisyllable words appears in Item 1 of the section on pronunciation of multisyllable words, on page 82.) Words with a vowel team as the first-syllable vowel unit also follow these patterns (*neigh·bor, coun·try, shoul·der, laun·dry*).

When there is just a single-sound consonant team between the vowel units (*rather, siphon, bother*), it usually is not divided. These words must be analyzed according to the VCV pattern (below). Sometimes words with consonant blends also should be analyzed in this way, treating the consonant blend as if it were a single consonant (*su·crose*).

⬦ The VCV Pattern

The VCV pattern works like this: If the first syllable contains a single vowel (not a vowel-r unit or a vowel-team unit) and is followed by only one consonant before the next vowel unit, that first vowel can be long or short, or it can be schwa if the syllable is not accented:

$$\text{tīdal} \qquad\qquad \text{rĭver} \qquad\qquad \text{sǝcure}$$

There are two different ways to teach this structure; the teacher must decide which one to use:

1. Always divide the word between the first vowel and the consonant (*ti·dal, ri·ver, se·cure, si·phon, ra·ther*). The first syllable is then an open syllable, and the vowel may be long, short, or schwa. Sound out the word, trying the long vowel sound first (because it is the most common), and if that doesn't make a recognizable word, try the short

sound, and then the schwa. (Of course, the reader will only know what is right by recognizing the word from the sounds. Thus, when teaching this pattern, it is important to use words that are part of the student's listening vocabulary. When students I am teaching have tried all three vowel sounds and still don't recognize the word, I tell them which vowel sound to use and, when they have said the word, I pronounce it again, ask if they have heard the word before, and give a brief definition.)

2. First try dividing between the first vowel and the consonant (as in **1**); in this case, the first syllable will be open, so its vowel will have the long sound. Sound out the word using the long vowel sound and, if that produces a word you know, quit. If that doesn't produce a word you know, divide the word between the consonant and the second vowel (*riv·er, rath·er*); in this case, the first syllable will be closed, so its vowel will have the short sound. Try saying the word using the short vowel sound. If you recognize the word, quit. If not, try the schwa sound for the first vowel and shift your accent to the second syllable (*secure*). (Again, the only way the reader will know the correct sound for the word is by recognizing the word as it is sounded out.)

If the consonant between the vowels is an *r*, the sound of the first vowel is often that of the *-are, -ire, -ore, -ure,* and *-ere* units (*vary, zero, meri-, Sarah, jury*). In words of more than two syllables, the vowel before the *r* is often unstressed and therefore has the schwa sound (*em̲erald, app̲aratus*). Whether the *r* is put with the next syllable (*ap·pə·rat·us*) or kept with the schwa sound (*ap·pər·at·us*) really doesn't matter, as long as the word is recognizable when sounded out.

◈◈ Pronunciation of Multisyllable Words ◈◈

As was illustrated in the previous section, in addition to knowing ways of syllabicating words, a reader must know the logical vowel sounds to use when decoding multisyllables. Unfortunately, even more vowel-sound shifts are possible in multisyllable words than in monosyllables. Again, the sounds follow patterns, but there are many patterns that will need practice. Some of the patterns that will help readers pronounce unfamiliar words are listed here. These need not be memorized; they are supplied merely to illustrate the variety of sound patterns that occur in English.

1. The vowels before *r* are among the most variable in multisyllable words.

    (a) Usually, when a vowel-r unit is followed by another consonant and is in the accented syllable, it has the same sound as it would in a monosyllable; that is, it has the sound of a vowel-r-closed syllable (*parsimonious*, *portent*, *ornithology*).

    (b) When a vowel-r unit is followed by a *vowel* and is in the accented syllable, it will often have the sound it has in a vowel-r-magic-e syllable (*characterize*, *ethereal*, *Oregon*, *puritan*). In this pattern, the *e* also has the short sound (*sclerosis*, *sheriff*); this sound varies with regional dialect, sometimes being pronounced like the *a* in this pattern. The *i* changes to the short sound, as well (*iridescent*, *miracle*).

    (c) When a vowel-r unit is followed by another *r* and then a vowel (often *y*), the vowel-r unit will often have the same sound as if it were followed by a vowel, as in the preceding case (*marry*, *berry*, *sorry*).

    (d) When the vowel before the *r* is in an unaccented syllable, the *vr* unit will have the /ər/ sound when followed by a consonant (*bifurcation*) or when followed by another *unaccented* syllable (*corporal*). If the unaccented syllable containing the vowel before *r* is followed by an *accented* syllable, the vowel still has the schwa sound, but the *r* is considered to be part of the accented syllable (*director* = də·rek′·tər).

You may have noticed that some people pronounce these vowel-r units slightly differently, depending on the word (contrast *Mary*, *merry*, and *marry*). These slight differences do not matter when teaching these decoding skills. Additionally, you have probably recognized that the *o* and *u* vary the least. As with many other patterns in multisyllable words, these vowel-r patterns are most easily taught by having the students practice on word lists organized by their spellings and sounds.

2. The *y* usually says /ē/ at the end of multisyllable words (*baby*, *artery*, *parsimony*). However:

    (a) the suffix *-fy* says /fī/ (*satisfy*, *magnify*, *diversify*);

    (b) the (few) *y*-ending words that are accented on the last syllable end with the /ī/ sound (*apply*, *rely*, *comply*, *awry*);

    (c) compound words that end with a *y*-ending monosyllabic word also give the *y* the /ī/ sound (*hereby*, *barfly*).

3. The *i* often says /ē/, especially when used as a connective (see the next paragraph) before suffixes (*-ia, -ium, -ial, -ient*, and so forth).

4. There are units called **connectives** that are very useful for identifying which syllables will be accented. The connectives are *i, u, ul*, and *ol*. They occur near the ends of words, connecting root words with suffixes, or connecting one suffix with another. The convenient thing about these connectives is that the syllable just before the connective is often the accented syllable, and there are certain patterns in which the syllable before the connective is virtually always accented. In the following examples, the connective is underlined and the accented syllable is marked: *co·me′di·an, man′u·al, stren′u·ous, trem′ul·ous.*

The connective *i* occurs most frequently, and it often occurs in a set of common suffixes: *-tion, -tial, -tious, -tient, -tience, -cian, -cial, -cient, -cious, -sion,* etc. The syllable just before these suffixes is the accented syllable, and if it is an open syllable, the vowel sounds are predictable: *a, o,* and *u* are long, *i* is short, and *e* (which seldom occurs) can be either long or short (*va·ca′tion, dis·tri·bu′tion, am·bi′tious, spe′cial*). Any other syllable preceding the connective has its usual vowel sound—if the syllable preceding the connective is closed, the vowel will be short (*sub·stan′tial*); if that syllable is a vowel-r-closed syllable, it will have the appropriate vowel-r sound (*com·mer′cial*); and so forth.

When *-ity* is added to words ending in one of these suffixes, the primary accent occurs just before the *-ity*; the previously accented syllable now receives the secondary accent (*par′tial,* but *par′ti·al′i·ty*).

Exercise 4.5   Study the list, WORDS ENDING IN A SUFFIX USING THE CONNECTIVE "I," on page 84, by reading the words aloud, listening for the stress patterns and vowel sounds.

5. The *-oon, -een,* and *-eer* syllables are accented:

    bal·loon′   ba·boon′   be·tween′   ca·reen′   en·gi·neer′   auc·tion·eer′

6. In words ending in *-ology,* the *ol* syllable is accented:

    a·pol′o·gy   *neu·ro·path·ol′o·gy*

7. When the suffix *-ic* is added to a word, the accent is on the syllable preceding that of the suffix:

    e·co·nom′ic   cat·a·clys′mic   al·pha·bet′ic   ath·let′ic

WORDS ENDING IN A SUFFIX USING THE CONNECTIVE "I"

Notice that the connective *i* plus the preceding letter say /sh/. The syllable (and vowel) just before the suffix is accented and those vowel sounds are very predictable. Listen to the rhythm of the words and the vowel preceding the suffix as you say them.

car na tion

a bra sion

com mo tion

e mo tion

ex plo sion

so lu tion

con clu sion

in fu sion

ad di tion

am bi tion

e di tion

ig ni tion

col li sion

di vi sion

con trap tion

de scrip tion

per fec tion

ex ten sion

a dop tion

com pul sion

as ser tion

im mer sion

ex cur sion

con tor tion

Con fu cian

Cau ca sian

bi ra cial

au da cious

vor a tious

a tro cious

fe ro cious

phy si cian

of fi cial

su spi cion

re li gion

re li gious

ma li cious

am bi tious

fi nan cial

pro vin cial

un con scious

in fec tious

ram bunc tious

ob nox ious

con sor tia

com mer cial

i ner tial

im par tial

aug men ta tion

ex pla na tion

i so la tion

lo co mo tion

con vo lu tion

dis il lu sion

mal oc clu sion

ac qui si tion

com pe ti tion

de fi ni tion

ex tra di tion

su per sti tion

in de ci sion

tel e vi sion

in ter ac tion

sat is fac tion

con tra dic tion

in ter mis sion

im per fec tion

hy per ten sion

in ter rup tion

mis con struc tion

dis pro por tion

re ap por tion

An a sta sia

hy per pla sia

in ter fa cial

an ti so cial

per ti na cious

os ten ta tious

the o lo gian

Lil li pu tian

e lec tri cian

pol i ti cian

ar ti fi cial

in ter sti tial

a va ri cious

in ju di cious

sac ri le gious

ad ven ti tious

co ef fi cient

or tho don tia

cir cum stan tial

ev i den tial

in flu en tial

con sci en tious

un pre ten tious

non com mer cial

Hundreds of words follow these patterns, most ending in -*tion*. Words with four or more syllables have a variety of secondary accent patterns: e.g.,

ac com' mo da' tion, im' ple men ta' tion, mis rep' re sen ta' tion

Reading lists of these words organized by accent patterns provides relatively easy practice on the rhythm of multisyllabic words.

8. In words ending in *-graphy*, the syllable that includes the *g* is accented:

   de·mog'ra·phy   bib·li·og'ra·phy   te·leg'ra·phy   cal·lig'ra·phy

If *-ic* is added to these words, the accent shifts to to *graph*, the syllable preceding *-ic*:

   bib·li·o·graph'ic   tel·e·graph'ic   hor·e·o·graph'ic

9. In words ending in *-otic* and *-osis*, the syllable containing the *o* of this ending is virtually always accented:

   cha·ot'ic   nar·cot'ic   os·mo'sis   di·ag·no'sis   hyp·no'sis

There are alternative pronunciations for *metamorphosis*:

   met·a·mor'pho·sis and *met·a·mor·pho'sis*

Interestingly, the *o* in *-osis* is usually long, while the *o* in *-otic* is usually short:

   psychōsis, but *psychŏtic*;   *neurōsis*, but *neurŏtic*

When these patterns are taught to students who have difficulty learning to decode, the students should *not* memorize a list of these rules. Rather, they work on the patterns and the rhythms of the words by using word lists and reading the words in sentences.[1]

Exercise 4.6   From a page in a book or magazine, rewrite all multisyllable words, dividing the words into syllables. Place the accent marks and put the proper diacritical marks above all vowel units.

---

[1]Lists of multisyllable words, organized according to syllable and accent patterns, are available from Oxton House, Publishers.

V

Phonemic Awareness

Up until the past decade, books on phonics have talked only about the sounds for letters and letter units. Now, much emphasis is placed on the understanding and teaching of "phonemic awareness," the ability to manipulate the individual sounds of spoken words. This shift in emphasis has come about as a result of research into the characteristics and problems of the large number of children in our schools who do not learn to read at an acceptable level. Estimates of the percentage of reading failures in the nation have run consistently at about 25%; this is particularly puzzling because the majority of children learn to read regardless of the teaching methods used by their teachers.

The search for causes for this relatively high rate of reading failure has led to a huge body of research, some of it dating from the nineteenth century. Major theories about reading disabilities that prevailed from the 1920s into the 1970s assumed that the difficulties lay in the realms of visual perception, visual-motor integration, or auditory perception, but subsequent research has not supported these assumptions. Interestingly, a number of the professionals who investigated the auditory perceptual characteristics of poor readers observed and accurately described some of the major problems encountered in the early stages of reading; however, attributing those problems to the auditory perception process led many researchers and teachers in the wrong direction.

⊗ **Identifying the Problem** ⊗

Linguists describe four separate areas of functioning in the human language system: phonology, syntax, semantics, and pragmatics. **Phonology** deals with the sound patterns of a language. As we put our ideas into words, it is the phonological part of our language system that assembles the proper sounds of those words in the proper sequence. About twenty-five years ago, Isabelle Liberman hypothesized that the primary basis for difficulty in learning to read an alphabetic written language is rooted in the cognitive area of language, and within the language system it is in the area of phonology. Since an alphabetic writing system uses symbols to represent the sounds of a language, readers must understand that words can be segmented into sounds in order to understand why we put the same basic set of letters together in an enormous variety of sequences. Only then can they understand that *stake* and *skate*, for instance, have the same letters, but they represent different words because the sequence of the letters—and therefore the sequence of the sounds—is different.[1] To those of us who are proficient readers this seems very elementary and, indeed, so easy to understand as to be silly to even worry about; however, the ability to do this is not at all easy for young children, and remains difficult—often into adulthood—for a number of people. In the last twenty years, a large body of research has demonstrated that this ability to segment words into sounds is the basic test of learning to read in an alphabetic reading system such as English. The degree to which pre-readers are aware of the individual sounds in spoken words predicts future reading success better than any other characteristic we can measure—better than intelligence, better than parents' educational background, better than visual or auditory perception, better than memory, even better than eyesight.

Since the early 1970s, Liberman and many of her colleagues and students have investigated a variety of questions that result from her hypothesis. This research has involved children who are pre-readers, beginning readers, or proficient readers, as well as literate and illiterate adults, in both English- and non-English-speaking countries. The results have contributed greatly to our understanding of oral language and the way in which it relates to

---

[1]People need not be consciously aware of the individual sounds within words to be expert *speakers* of a language. In oral language, words and phrases are meaningful units as wholes; it is distracting to focus on the individual sounds. Only when we need to understand the representation of thousands of different words by only a small number of written symbols must we focus on the individual sounds that these symbols represent.

alphabetic and syllabic written languages. For example, it has become clear that there are different levels of conscious awareness of the phonology of words:

- Awareness of phonological strings, a global awareness that allows us to tell when phonological strings (words or just strings of sounds pronounced like words) are the same or different, as in detecting or producing rhymes. This is called **phonological awareness**.

- Awareness of syllables, which implies the more analytic ability to segment connected speech into syllables.

- Awareness of phonemes, which implies the analytic ability to segment syllables into separate phonemes and manipulate those phonemes. This is what has come to be called **phonemic awareness**.

- Awareness of phonetic features, which implies the ability to analyze and compare the features of individual phonemes.

The term "awareness" in "phonemic awareness" is not a very good descriptor of the kinds of activities that demonstrate the level of phoneme cognizance meant by phonemic awareness. The skill required at this level is truly analytic; it involves being able to segment words into separate phonemes and to manipulate those phonemes. For example, we might ask a student to say *fit*, and then to say it without the /f/; the student has to segment the word minimally into /f/ and /it/ in order to delete the first sound. Or we might ask a student to say *fit*, and then to say it with /z/ instead of /t/; the student has to segment the word to isolate the /t/ sound and then replace this sound with /z/ when saying the word. Early researchers examined a wide variety of phonological activities and used various terms to label the types of skills they were investigating. Gradually, it has become clear that these activities delineate different levels of awareness of sounds, such as the four described above. Even now, however, the precise assignment to these levels of the various activities that fit somewhere between phonological awareness and phonemic awareness is not entirely clear. Nevertheless, it is clear that phonemic awareness activities fit into a relatively sophisticated level, one that requires the analytic abilities of segmentation and manipulation of phonemes, not simply the recognition of different sound patterns. Perhaps, as these concepts and activities become widely known, a more descriptive word (such as "manipulation") will replace "awareness" in phonemic awareness. Until then, we need to be aware that there is an important, if subtle, distinction between "phonological awareness" and "phonemic awareness."

As the research has shown, children under the age of five can commonly do tasks that tap awareness of phonological strings and can relatively easily be taught to do tasks that show awareness of syllables; however, they cannot often complete tasks that demonstrate awareness of phonemes. Early research also showed that the ability to complete phonological awareness activities strongly predicts later reading and spelling achievement. Furthermore, by the end of first grade, good readers generally display good phonemic awareness and poor readers generally do not. This body of research led to two questions that are crucial for parents, child-care providers, nursery school, kindergarten, and primary grade teachers:

> Can phonological awareness and phonemic awareness skills be taught to children? If so, will these skills help the children learn to read an alphabetic written language such as English?

Research has demonstrated that the answer to both questions is an emphatic *Yes*.

Several different research studies have compared the achievement of children who have received training on a variety of phonological awareness and phonemic awareness tasks, and also on letter ⇔ sound correspondences. These research studies have demonstrated that children who have been specifically taught phonemic awareness tasks in kindergarten (e.g., syllable segmenting and sound reversal tasks) significantly outperform untrained children in reading and spelling during the primary grades, and that training in phonemic awareness *and* letter ⇔ sound correspondences produces superior learning to training in either skill alone. Furthermore, a long-term study conducted in England demonstrated that if children who have poor phonological awareness when they are four years old[2] were specifically trained on both phonemic awareness tasks and letter ⇔ sound correspondences when they were five and six years old, their reading and spelling skills became significantly superior to those of similar children who were taught to analyze the *meanings* of words and to children who did not receive any special training at all. When these children were 13 years old, they were retested in reading and spelling. The advantage of the group trained in phonemic awareness and letter ⇔ sound correspondences was maintained over this long period of time, and many children who did not receive this training were now two years or more behind the trained children in reading, even though some of them had received remedial reading services for several years.

---

[2]Based on previous research findings, such children were expected to have difficulty learning to read.

⧉ Developing Phonemic Awareness ⧉

We now know that phonological awareness is a crucial skill for preschool children to acquire and that phonemic awareness is every bit as crucial for a beginning reader. Moreover, we know a number of ways to help children develop these skills. Preschool children should learn nursery rhymes, especially those in which the rhymes are the most obvious feature of the poem. If the poems are sometimes recited with a great deal of vocal emphasis on the words that rhyme, the children's attention will be drawn to the rhyme. (Children whose phonological language system is developing normally are usually able to detect rhyme as young as three years of age, but children with problems in phonological awareness often have great difficulty with this when they are four and five years old.) Eventually the children should be able to rhyme words. Siegfried Engelmann recommended using multisyllable words at the beginning of this type of rhyming activity and encouraging children to be funny with the words they make up to rhyme. For example, if you start with *hamburger*, change it to *lambburger*, and then to *famburger*, suggesting that the child make up some silly words that end the same, even young children for whom this is relatively difficult will often begin to rhyme such words. I have found that multisyllable words ending in a shorter word that the children know makes it easiest for them at the beginning of this game (e.g., *bicycle, tricycle, mycycle, hicycle*, or *skateboard, fateboard*, and so on). Gradually, most children learn to rhyme monosyllabic words, too.

Other good activities for preschool children to work on include identifying pictures for which the beginning sound or the beginning consonant and vowel sound of the name of the pictures is the same. For example, given pictures of a *pig*, a *pin*, a *pit*, and a *sun* (or *pig, pen, pot*, and *sun*), the child might put the *pig, pin*, and *pit* pictures together, or might tell which picture doesn't fit. When children can do this easily with pictures, they can often just listen to three or four words and tell which ones go together, or which one doesn't fit with the rest. This can also be done with the middle sounds of words (*pat, sad, lap, sit*), and with the ending sounds (*sat, fit, lot, rug*), though ending sounds seem to be more difficult for many children.

Many skill-development activities can take the form of games or puzzles and can be used by teachers or parents in an informal, recreational setting. The rest of this chapter is devoted to describing some of these activities, assuming that you, the reader, are playing the role of the "coach."

While taking a long car trip, for instance, the game of looking for things whose names start with a particular sound can keep children amused for a long time while practicing a very important phonological skill. Extra challenge and interest can be added by working through the alphabet, finding one thing that starts with /ā/ or /ă/, then /b/, etc.; often you will need to say the next sound, and will have to specify the long or short vowel sound, unless the child can handle an either/or choice. If you play this game with your children, you'll have to decide what to do with *c* and *x*; if your children don't know the sequence of the alphabet, it won't matter whether you include them or not; if they do, you can decide together what to do, talking about the sound as you decide.

A similar game is "I Spy," using a specified sound for the choice. As a teacher or parent, you might say, "I spy something that begins with the sound /m/," or "...that ends with the sound /t/," etc., choosing word-parts and sounds that your child can handle without too much difficulty. There are also the games in which each player has to think of a word beginning with the next letter of the alphabet. They begin with a variety of sentences, such as:

I went to my grandmother's attic and found a ____,

or

I went to my uncle's store and bought a ____.

Many four-, five-, and six-year-old children can play this with help. It is often played as a memory game, by having each player repeat all of the items named previously; with young children or children with memory problems, help must be given in a manner that does not belittle the child who needs it.

Children also enjoy counting the number of syllables in words that are pronounced for them. "Counting" can be done in a variety of ways with young children, such as clapping, tapping the table or the knee, or holding up fingers for each syllable. For some reason, it seems to be hardest for children to "count" the syllable in a one-syllable word, so I preface such words with a comment indicating that the next one will be different and they should think carefully (e.g., "Here's a tricky one" or "Be careful with this one"). Children enjoy clapping out names of people they know, and they quickly get good enough to tackle long words such as *abracadabra* and *supercalifragilisticexpialidocious*.

As children get proficient at completing these activities by which they are asked to recognize how the sound segments in words differ, they can begin doing activities that ask them to manipulate the sounds themselves. For example, you can give them a word to say (e.g., *fit*) and then have them say it without the /f/. For children who have difficulty with this, you can begin with compound words, having them leave off one of the syllables; for example:

"Say *toothpaste.* ... Say it without *tooth.*"

or

"Say *toothpaste.* ... Say it without *paste.*"

When omitting a sound is mastered, have the children substitute a sound for the one you specify:

"Say *mad.* ... Now change the /m/ to /s/."

Work gradually on beginning, middle, and ending sounds.

When the children become comfortable with manipulating the sounds in words, begin to use colored chips or small pieces of paper to represent the sounds. Each different sound should be represented with a different color, but the same color does not always have to match a particular sound. For example, if you have red, yellow, green, blue, and purple chips, *map* could be red-yellow-green, or blue-green-purple, or yellow-purple-blue. A word like *dad* could be red-yellow-red, or green-blue-green, or purple-blue-purple, with both *d*'s the same color. Give the child problems to solve that require manipulating the colors to represent the sounds. For example, put out two chips of different colors and say:

"If this says /ĭt/, make it say /ĭf/" (expecting the student to replace the second chip with one of another color);

or

"If this says / īp/, make it say /āp/" (expecting the student to replace the first chip).

You can also also have them delete a sound:

"If this says /ăt/, make it say /ă/."

also, have the child build the "words":

"Show me one that says /dā/ (/tā/, /fī/, /ĭd/, /ŏp/, ...)."

Move to three-letter "words" and try having the child be the teacher, telling you what to do. When the children have learned the sounds for some consonants and a vowel, they can use letter cards or tiles for these activities, and they will be reading and spelling words!

A number of more challenging variations of the game "I am thinking of something that ____" or "I spy something that ____" can be played by giving the sequence of sounds that make a word; for example:

"I am thinking of doing something that has the sounds /ē/ /t/";

"I can see something that has the sounds /k/ /ă/ /t/";

"I spy something that has the sounds /f/ /ā/ /s/."

The words chosen can be varied in length and difficulty to suit a child's individual needs, abilities, and interests.

The "secret" languages that many school-aged children enjoy learning require good phonemic awareness skills. For instance, Pig Latin requires that words beginning with consonants have the initial consonant (or consonant-team) sound moved to the end of the word and followed by the sound /ā/; words beginning with vowels have /wā/ added to them. Thus,

"I like that green jacket"

becomes

"I-wā ike-lā at-thā een-grā acket-jā."

Children who develop good phonemic awareness skills easily can learn to use this language by listening to it being used and repeating some of the words they hear. However, children who must be taught phonemic awareness skills explicitly would need quite a bit of instruction and guided practice on words. The advantage of using Pig Latin (or some similar code language) is that phonemic awareness can be practiced within the context of ordinary communication.

All of these activities help the children with the blending they will do when reading words and the segmenting they will do when spelling. When spelling a word that is not memorized, children segment the word into its sounds and then write the letter(s) for each sound. For example, *lap* becomes /l/ (write the *l*), /ă/ (write the *a*), /p/ (write the *p*). To see how this works for adults, write *phonological* and listen to what you are thinking (saying) while you write. You will segment the word into its syllables and write each syllable as you say it. Children gradually move from working with one sound at a time to working with a syllable at a time as they become automatic at writing syllables without segmenting them. The emphasis on having very young children express themselves in writing, using invented spellings, has added excellent phonemic-awareness practice to classroom activities. The children sound out the words they want to write and put down symbols—including any letters they know—for the sounds.

When reading a word that is not recognized by sight (i.e., by just look-ing at the word and saying it all at once), children need to be able to say the phonemes for the graphemes in order, blend those sounds into a sound stream, and then recognize the word in their own vocabulary that matches that sound stream. With the sounds that are continuants (e.g., /m/, /s/, /f/, and the vowels), the blended sound stream sounds like the word: the sounds /m/, /a/, and /n/ can be run right into each other, sounding like the word *man*. With stopped sounds (e.g., /b/, /d/, /p/, /t/), the sound stream will not sound just like the word, no matter how fast the sounds are pronounced (/p/ /ă/ /t/), even if the vowel and ending consonant are pronounced together (/p/ /ăt/).

For children who have a learning disability in reading-decoding, or dyslexia, recognizing the word that matches the sound stream can be a very difficult task. All of the activities that develop phonemic awareness will help to get them ready for this task, but those activities will often be very difficult and might be met with much resistance. It is important to find at least one activity that meets with some success to begin developing phonological awareness and then gradually move through more activities to develop phonemic awareness, acknowledging that this is difficult and requires hard work and giving lots of compliments when the child does work hard at the tasks. At the beginning of each different activity, you will often need to lead the child through each response, essentially saying the answer with the child. You are providing a model for the child, and will need to keep doing this until the child starts responding well enough for you to drop out. I find that working with syllables of multisyllable words before moving to individual phonemes helps the children understand what I am asking them to do, thereby making the task a little easier. However, the disability seems to be focused on the part of the language system that deals with individual phonemes, and the only way to overcome it is to work explicitly on developing those skills that seem to develop so readily in children without this disability.

The list of activities described in this section certainly is not exhaustive. The section on phonological and phonemic awareness in the Suggestions for Further Reading (on page 137) provides references for more activities and for more details on the activities suggested here.

Appendix A

Sounds for Consonants and Vowels

∞⤫∞⤫∞⤫∞⤫∞⤫∞⤫∞⤫∞⤫∞⤫∞⤫∞⤫∞⤫∞⤫∞⤫∞⤫∞⤫∞⤫∞

⟨⟨⟨⟩ Consonants and Consonant Teams ⟨⟨⟨⟩

The information in this section can be used to learn the sounds for the single consonants, the single-sound consonant teams, and the consonant blends. If you are teaching this information to a beginning reader, introduce only a few graphemes at a time, making sure that your student can give the correct sounds for almost all the graphemes already covered before you introduce more. Some research studies have looked at whether it is better to teach the common sounds for a grapheme one at a time or all at once; the results indicate that it is best to introduce all of the sounds for a grapheme at the same time, even if you might initially use only one of the sounds in words. Having done this for years, I find that it works much better than teaching and using only one sound at a time. Thus, when you introduce sounds for a vowel, teach the long, short, and schwa sounds (e.g., /ā/, /ă/, and ə) right away; when you introduce c, teach both phonemes (/k/ and /s/). Do not teach the generalizations that go with the graphemes (e.g., c ⇒ /s/ before e, i, and y) when you teach the sounds; teach these generalizations only as they are needed to read or spell words.

The consonant lists indicate which sounds are voiced and which are unvoiced. **Voiced sounds** are those for which the vocal cords, as well as the mouth and lips, are used to make the sound. When you are saying a voiced sound, you can feel your vocal cords vibrate if you touch the sides of your Adam's apple at the top of your throat as you speak. For example, say "z-z-z-z-z-z" while touching the sides of your Adam's apple; you should feel

your vocal cords vibrate. Now say "ssssss"; you won't feel any vibration because /s/ is an unvoiced sound. **Unvoiced sounds** are made by pushing air
through the mouth, opened to varying degrees, with the tongue, teeth, and
lips in a variety of positions. Many voiced consonant sounds are matched
with unvoiced sounds. For example, the unvoiced /s/ uses the same mouth
and lip formation as the voiced /z/. Similarly, the sound /g/ is voiced and
/k/ is its matching unvoiced sound. This matching is illustrated by the
vertical pairing of the voiced and unvoiced consonant sounds in Table 3.

Voiced:	b	d	g	j	l	m	n	r	v	w	y	z					th(e)
Unvoiced:	p	t	k	ch					f	wh		s	h	x	sh	th(in)

Voiced and unvoiced sounds.

Table 3

Children do not need to learn explicitly which sounds are voiced and
which are unvoiced, but they usually enjoy comparing them. What is important is that beginning readers of any age pronounce the sounds correctly,
and that they know which graphemes spell the sounds they are making.
Comparing voiced and unvoiced sounds often makes it easier to remember
how to say the sounds correctly because the extra focus on articulation adds
another mnemonic cue that helps the reader learn the important features
of the phoneme. When the sounds are practiced, they should be as short
and precise as possible, with no more of an attached schwa sound than is
absolutely necessary. The unvoiced sounds should not have any schwa sound
(or any other voiced sound) attached at all.

Some sounds are called "continuants" and some are said to be "stopped."
Continuants are sounds that can be produced continuously for as long as
your breath lasts (e.g., /s/, /z/, /f/, /v/, /m/, /n/, and vowels). **Stopped
sounds** cannot be drawn out like that, but are made with a single burst
of breath as a stoppage in the air passage is released (e.g., /t/, /b/, /k/,
/p/). It is usually easier for young children, and for any students who have
difficulty recognizing a word from its sounds, to start reading by decoding
words that begin with continuants (e.g., /s/ /a/ /t/ rather than /b/ /a/ /t/).
Because of this, many phonics programs begin by teaching the sounds for
the continuants *s*, *m*, and *f*, along with *t* and *a*; these are followed soon
after by *n*, along with *b* and *p*. By using this order, teachers and students
can build a lot of words that are familiar even to very young children. (It
is not particularly useful to teach the terms "continuant" and "stopped" to
students, but it is useful to talk about how the sounds are made.)

⊗ Single Consonants

b ⇒ /b/ (*bat*), voiced; *b* after *m* in the same syllable is silent (*lamb*).

c ⇒ /k/ before *a*, *o*, *u*, and all consonants except *h*, and at the end of multisyllable words (*cat, topic*), unvoiced; called the hard sound.

⇒ /s/ before *e*, *i*, and *y* (*city*), unvoiced; called the soft sound.

d ⇒ /d/ (*dog*), voiced.

f ⇒ /f/ (*fat*), unvoiced; usually doubled right after a short vowel at the end of monosyllables (*cliff*).

g ⇒ /g/ before *a*, *o*, *u*, and consonants (*game*), voiced; called the hard sound.

⇒ /j/ before *e*, *i*, and *y* (*gem*), voiced; called the soft sound. This pattern is not as regular as the corresponding *c* pattern (e.g., *get, give,* and *girl* should have the soft /j/ sound, but they don't).

h ⇒ /h/ (*hat*), unvoiced. Sometimes the *h* is silent (*honesty, hour*); this varies to a certain degree, often with regional dialect (e.g., *huge* is pronounced both with and without the /h/).

j ⇒ /j/ (*jam*), voiced. See also *g* and *-dge*.

k ⇒ /k/ (*kit*), unvoiced; used before *e*, *i*, and *y*. See also *c*, *-ck*, *ch*, and *qu*.

l ⇒ /l/ (*lap*), voiced. The /l/ sound at the beginning of words is started with the tongue on the roof of the mouth, and it glides into the vowel sound. In isolation, this sound would be /lə/. At the end of words, we glide from the previous vowel to the /l/ (*seal, hill*). In isolation, this sound would be /ᵛl/, with the ᵛ vowel sound often becoming a diphthong (/ā-əl/ in *pail*, /ē-əl/ in *seal*). Because this is confusing for spelling, I teach students to say /lə/ for *l-* and the blends (*bl-, gl-,* etc.) and /əl/ for *-l* and the *-cle* syllables, keeping the schwa part of the sound as short as possible.

m ⇒ /m/ (*mat*), voiced.

n ⇒ /n/ (*nap*), voiced. See also *gn, kn,* and *pn*.

p ⇒ /p/ (*pat*), unvoiced.

r ⇒ /r/ (*rat*), voiced. After a vowel, the *r* creates a vowel-r syllable and changes the vowel sound. The *r-* should be taught as /rə/, rather than as /ər/, for the beginnings of words (*rail*) and in blends (*grade*).

s ⇒ /s/ (*sit*), unvoiced; usually doubled immediately after a short vowel at the end of a monosyllable (*miss, pass*).

⇒ /z/ (*has*), voiced; usually the sound for a single *s* at the end of a monosyllable and in some multisyllable words, but with some common exceptions: *bus, gas, Gus, sis* (which are shortened forms of other words); *pus, this, thus, us,* and *yes.*

t ⇒ /t/ (*tap*), unvoiced; sometimes silent when *t* starts a new syllable and *s* ends the syllable before it (*hasten, whistle*).

v ⇒ /v/ (*van*), voiced. English words ending with the /v/ sound are always spelled with -*ve.*

w ⇒ /w/ (*wet*), voiced; *w* before a single *a* usually, but not always, modifies the vowel sound (*wash*, but *wax*); *w* before *ar* and *or* modifies their sounds (*war, work*); *w* following a vowel substitutes for *u*, creating a vowel team (*how, threw, saw*); occasionally, *u* substitutes for *w* as a consonant (*suave*).

x ⇒ /ks/ (*box*), unvoiced; acts like two consonants for adding endings (*boxes*) and for syllable division (*axle*).

⇒ /gs/ (*exact*), voiced; also acts like two consonants for syllable division.

⇒ /z/ (*xylophone*), voiced.

y ⇒ /y/ as a consonant (*yet*), voiced. It is a consonant only when it is the first letter of a syllable.

⇒ As a vowel, it takes the sound and place of *i* (*gym, cycle, fly, play*) and usually says /ē/ at the end of multisyllable words. Like all vowels, it is voiced.

z ⇒ /z/ (*zip*), voiced; usually doubled immediately after a short vowel at the end of a monosyllable (*jazz*).

❈ Single-Sound Consonant Teams

The order in which the single-sound consonant teams are introduced usually depends largely on their usefulness for reading sentences and stories that are appropriate for the student. Some very useful teams are used in many words (e.g., *sh*); some are used in fewer words, but in words that occur frequently (e.g., *wh* in *which, when, where, what,* and *why*). The order in which they are presented here should not be viewed as the only correct order, but should be varied with the reading needs of particular students.

The teams with a silent letter are particularly difficult for many students to remember; I put a slash through the silent letter (e.g., *gn, wr*) and let them practice with this form for as long as it takes to become automatic at saying the correct sound. Since these teams are not used very commonly, there is no sense in spending a lot of time and energy on them.

qu ⇒ /kw/ (*quit*); the /k/ is unvoiced, but the /w/ is voiced. As /kw/, the *qu* should properly be categorized as a blend, rather than as a SSCT, because the *q* has its normal /k/ sound and the *u* has the sound of *w* (as it sometimes has following a consonant). Traditionally, however, *qu* has been called a digraph, which would make it a SSCT. This makes better pedagogical sense, since it needs to be taught early, well before students would know that *u* sometimes says *w*. When it appears before a single *a*, *ar*, and *or*, it modifies their sounds in the same way that *w* does.

⇒ /k/ (*conquer*), unvoiced; occurs in *antique, plaque*, and other French words.

-ck ⇒ /k/ (*back*), unvoiced; used at the end of monosyllables immediately after a short vowel.

sh ⇒ /sh/ (*shut*), unvoiced.

ch ⇒ /ch/ (*chip*), unvoiced.

⇒ /k/ (*chorus*), unvoiced.

⇒ /sh/ (*machine*), unvoiced.

-tch ⇒ /ch/ (*catch*), unvoiced; used at the end of monosyllables immediately after a short vowel.

th ⇒ /th/, both voiced, (as in *then*) and unvoiced (as in *thick*).

wh ⇒ /wh/ (*which*), unvoiced. It is difficult to distinguish /wh/ from /w/ (*witch*), so I teach students to blow as they make the /wh/; then, by holding a finger in front of their lips, they can feel the difference between /w/ and /wh/.

ph ⇒ /f/ (*phone*), unvoiced. Words containing the *ph* grapheme are from the Greek language.

-dge ⇒ /j/ (*fudge*), voiced; used at the end of monosyllables immediately after a short vowel.

-ng ⇒ /ng/ (*bang*), voiced.

-nk ⇒ /nk/ (*bank*), voiced.

(The phonemes /ng/ and /nk/ are difficult for some children; they can be practiced as *ang, ing, ong, ung,* and *ank, ink, onk, unk.*)

kn ⇒ /n/ (*knit*), voiced.

gn ⇒ /n/ (*gnat*), voiced.

pn ⇒ /n/ (*pneumonia*), voiced.

gh ⇒ /g/ at the beginning of syllables (*ghost*), voiced; often silent after vowels (*light, sleigh*).

wr ⇒ /r/ (*write*), voiced.

ps- ⇒ /s/ (*psalm*), unvoiced; at the beginnings of words.

sc ⇒ /s/ before *e*, *i*, and *y* (*science*), unvoiced.

(The grapheme *sc* before *a*, *o*, *u*, and consonants is a consonant blend, as described below.)

-mb ⇒ /m/ (*limb*), voiced.

◈ Consonant Blends

The consonant blends just combine the regular sounds that each single letter or consonant team has in isolation. Once students are automatic at giving the sounds for single consonants and the more common single-sound consonant teams, I begin teaching the consonant blends. Students practice pronouncing the blends and writing the letters as the blends are pronounced. They could sound out words and spell them by treating each letter and sound separately, but this approach would put an unnecessary burden on sequential memory and on blending skills. (For instance, *stand* would require that five separate sounds be remembered in the correct sequence for blending and for spelling.) If, instead, students become automatic at saying /st/ when they see *st* and at writing *st* when they hear /st/, and become similarly proficient with the other consonant blends, then almost all syllables will have only two or three units to be remembered and sequenced correctly (e.g., *a·nd, str·e·tch, fl·i·nt*).[1] Students quickly and easily become automatic at writing and giving sounds for consonant blends, so it is well worth taking the time to practice the blends as single units. I usually start by teaching the <u>c</u>l blends, then proceed in order to *nd* and *nt*, the <u>c</u>r group, the s<u>c</u> group, and then the others, as quickly as the students can master them.

---

[1] Three exceptions are *l·e·ng·th, str·e·ng·th,* and *tw·e·lf·th*.

The consonant blends are listed here in words that typify their occurrences. Some that are used only in one or two words (e.g., *next*) are omitted.

black *cling* *flop* *glad* *plus* *slide* *brain* *crayon* *drop* *fresh*
press *trip* *scale* *skip* *brisk* *slot* *small* *snoop* *spunk* *gasp*
staid *rusty* *swing* *twice* *squint* *splat* *scrub* *sprout* *strap*
shrug *thrice* *chrysalis* *send* *scent* *bunch* *stamp* *fact* *brisk*
left *help* *tilt* *opt*

❈ Other Letter Combinations

-aste ⇒ /āste/ (*paste*) and **ange** ⇒ /ānge/ (*range*), but **ance** ⇒ /ănce/ (*dance*); the rest of the vowels are short before *nge* and *nce* (*wince, lunge*); the *e* marks the *c* and *g*, keeping them soft.

-ble ⇒ /b'l/, **-cle** ⇒ /c'l/, **-dle** ⇒ /d'l/, etc. These are the *cle* syllables; they are pronounced with a slight schwa sound before the *l* (/əl/). To help with spelling, these should be contrasted with the *cl* blends (*bl, cl, fl, gl, pl, sl*), which sould be pronounced with the slight schwa sound after the *l* (/blə/, /clə/, /flə/, etc.).

❈ Vowels and Vowel Teams ❈

The mnemonic pictures that I use for teaching the sounds for the vowel teams appear on pages 104–109. Examples of words for each vowel and vowel team accompany the pictures. The examples are not meant to be memorized by the students; rather, they are presented to help you understand the vowel-sound patterns of English.

The pictures provide a visual memory device that helps students learn the large number of vowel teams and their varying sounds. Visualizing items in certain places is a powerful mnemonic tool for most people, and the pictures take advantage of that power. Students first memorize the placement of the letters on a picture; once they can reproduce the picture, they learn the sounds and diacritical marks for the vowel teams. If they forget the sound for a vowel team when they are reading, they can visualize the picture to help themselves retrieve it (or can be prompted by a question that will remind them to use the menemonic picture, such as "Where is the *au* on the skate?" or "Where is the *ou* on the ghost?"). Students also learn which letter combinations are used as vowel teams in English. This helps with spelling, since students will not try a letter combination (such as *ao* for /ā/) that they have not learned as a vowel team.

The vowel sounds are the most variable sounds in English. Each single vowel has more than one sound, as do many of the vowel teams. It is very important for students to practice giving all the sounds for a particular vowel unit and to practice words containing the different sounds, so that they can shift quickly from one sound to another when reading in context. Additionally, vowel sounds are affected by neighboring consonants and vary among regional dialects. When teaching decoding, it seems to be best if the patterns are kept as simple and straightforward as possible, which means that many of the fine gradations of sounds do not appear in the vowel sound patterns shown here. However, good readers need to be as flexible with sounds when they are reading as when they are speaking, so I do not ignore the subtle differences among sounds. I discuss the sound variations with my students and practice with lists of words that emphasize both the patterns and the variations. I often ask students to repeat a sentence after me in order that I may hear how they pronounce particular words, then use their pronunciation for discussion or for moving a word from one classification to another, such as moving *roof* from /rŏof/ to /rōof/. The following notes highlight a few specific sound variations as examples of patterns that deserve teachers' attention and often prompt students' questions.

For i:

- In multisyllable words, the *i* often has the sound /ē/: *machine, fatigue, lenient, opium, filial.* In words such as *variant* and *variable*, the ending *y* has been changed to *i* before the suffix, and the *i* uses the same /ē/ sound as the ending *y*.

For o:

- The letter combination *ou* followed by *gh* occurs in about two dozen words, with six different sounds, so I teach those words as sight words. Some of the more common ones are: *bought, fought, brought,* and *thought*; *cough*; *rough, tough,* and *enough*; *plough*; *dough, though,* and *thorough*; and *through*.

- In some regional dialects, the short *o* has a second pronunciation, /ô/, which is the same as the sound of *aw* and is used in words ending in *g* (e.g., *dog, fog, frog, log*). Some students who use this sound need to learn it explicitly; for them, there are two short *o* sounds, /ŏ/ and /ô/.

However, most students are able to adjust the sound appropriately as they sound out words, so they need only learn /ŏ/. When they sound out a word and don't seem to recognize it, I stop and discuss the variation in sound; usually, this is all that is needed.

- There are quite a few words in which *o* should have either a short sound (in an accented, closed syllable) or a long sound (in an accented, magic-e, or open syllable), but instead has a short *u* sound (e.g., *of, from, son, won, come, some, done, none, mother, honey, money*). Because these words are so common, I teach my students to try the "correct" sound first, and if that doesn't work, to try /ŭ/.

For **u**:

- There are really two sounds for the long *u*: the name of the letter (as in *use* and *cube*) and the /o͞o/ sound (as in *flute* and *prune*). I have found it unnecessary to teach both sounds explicitly. When sounding out words such as *flute*, *rude*, and *June*, a brief discussion of the use of /o͞o/ usually is sufficient for prompting the students to switch from /ū/ to /o͞o/. (In fact, they have fun trying to use /ū/ in those words!)

- The *ue* and *ui* both have the long *u* sound and do not occur in many words. I post the cube picture as a reference for the students, but I teach these letter combinations last. Most students do not need to memorize the picture and arc the vowel teams to learn these words.

  There are several words in which the *ue* or *ui* combination appears but is not used as a vowel team.

  – The *u* sometimes occurs as a silent letter after *b* or *g*, as in *build, buy, guess, guest, guild, guilt, guide, guile, guise, guy*, and *guitar*.

  – A silent marker *e* sometimes appears after *gu* at the end of a word, as in *vogue, morgue, fatigue*, and *catalogue*. In these cases, the final syllable of the word ends with a vowel, a consonant, and the (silent) *ue* (*vogue, -tigue*).

  – In some words, the *u* substitutes for the consonant *w*, as in *anguish, linguist*, and *unguent*.

- When *que* occurs at the end of a word, it usually (but not always) has the sound /k/ and behaves like a single-sound consonant team, as in *torque, mosque, antique*, and *critique*. In a few words, the *que* is a separate syllable: it has the sound /kā/ in *applique, risque*, and *communique*, and it has the sound /kē/ at the end of *Albuquerque*.

◈ The Vowel-Team Pictures

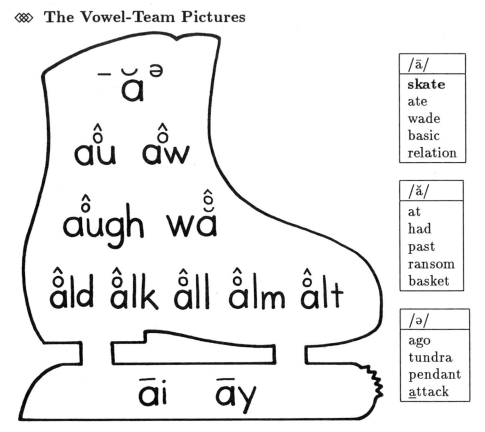

/ā/
skate
ate
wade
basic
relation

/ă/
at
had
past
ransom
basket

/ə/
ago
tundra
pendant
attack

ai	ay	au	aw	augh
aim	day	fault	saw	caught
braid	say	fraud	paw	taught
paint	play	gaunt	claw	daughter
twain	spray	launch	dawn	naughty
praise	tray	pause	crawl	haughty
Maine	Wayne	sauce	scrawl	slaughter

wa: /wô/	wa: /wă/	all	ald	alk	alm	alt
want	wax	ball	bald	talk	alms	halt
wash	wag	tall	scald	walk	calm	malt
swamp	swam	hall	alder	chalk	palm	salt
squash	twang	small	caldron	stalk	psalm	Walt
squat	quack					

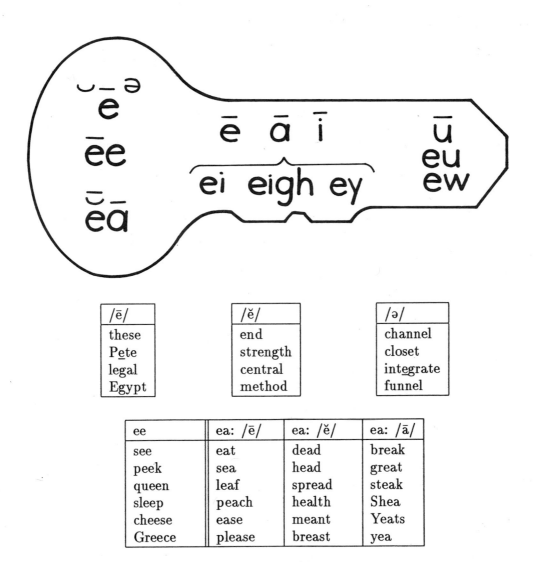

/ē/	/ĕ/	/ə/
these	end	channel
Pete	strength	closet
legal	central	integrate
Egypt	method	funnel

ee	ea: /ē/	ea: /ĕ/	ea: /ā/
see	eat	dead	break
peek	sea	head	great
queen	leaf	spread	steak
sleep	peach	health	Shea
cheese	ease	meant	Yeats
Greece	please	breast	yea

eu (ew): /ŭ/	ei (ey, eigh): /ā/	ei (ey, eigh): /ē/	ei (ey, eigh): /ī/
sleuth	veil	seize	heist
feud	beige	Keith	Heinz
deuce	they	**key**	eider
few	whey	money	eye
new	eight	valley	geyser
shrewd	weigh	Leigh	height

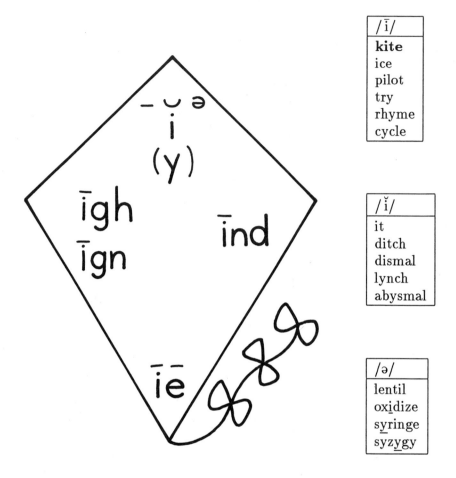

/ī/
kite
ice
pilot
try
rhyme
cycle

/ĭ/
it
ditch
dismal
lynch
abysmal

/ə/
lentil
oxidize
syringe
syzygy

ie: /ē/	i(y)e: /ī/	igh	ign	ind
brief	die	high	sign	bind
field	tie	thigh	align	kind
grieve	dye	night	assign	mind
piece	rye	flight	benign	grind
		wright		behind

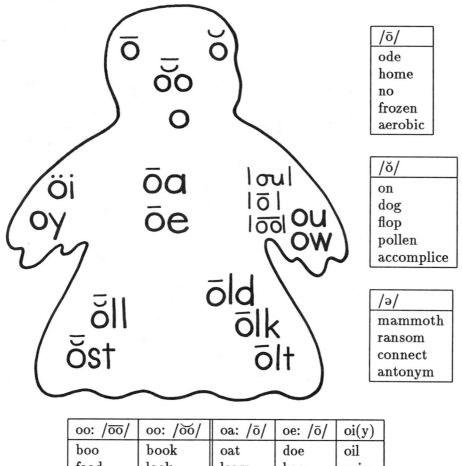

/ō/
ode
home
no
frozen
aerobic

/ŏ/
on
dog
flop
pollen
accomplice

/ə/
mammoth
ransom
connect
antonym

oo: /ōō/	oo: /ŏŏ/	oa: /ō/	oe: /ō/	oi(y)
boo	book	oat	doe	oil
food	look	loam	hoe	coin
smooth	good	groan	Joe	voice
moose	stood	loathe	throes	boy
Scrooge	oomph	loaves		ploy

old, olk, olt: /ō/	oll, ost: /ō/	oll, ost: /ŏ/	ou, ow: /ou/	ou, ow: /ō/	ou: /ōō/
gold	roll	doll	out	soul	you
scold	knoll	loll	round	poultry	soup
folk	scroll	Molly	bounce	own	group
yolk	**ghost**	cost	how	glow	rouge
bolt	most	lost	down	snow	
volt	post	frost	browse	owe	

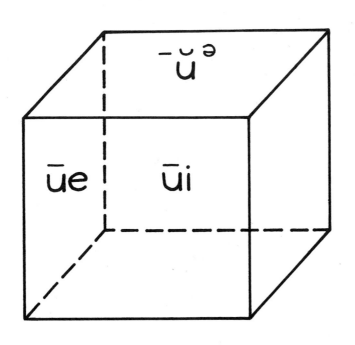

/ū/

cube
flute
emu
music
prune
student

/ŭ/

up
plush
funnel
penumbra

/ə/

crocus
spectrum
talcum
adjutant

ue: /ū/	ui: /ū/
cue	suit
due	fruit
hue	cruise
rue	juice
sue	sluice
blue	
clue	
flue	
glue	
true	

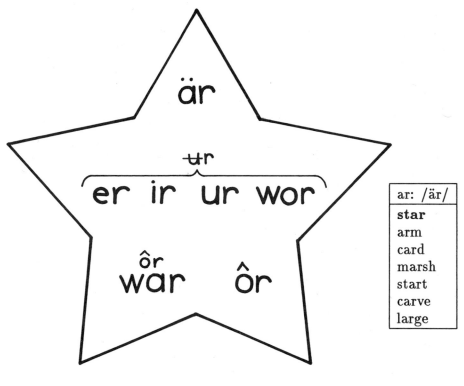

war: /ôr/	or: /ôr/	wor: /ʉr/	er: /ʉr/	ir: /ʉr/	ur: /ʉr/
war	born	word	Bert	bird	blur
warm	for	work	clerk	firm	church
dwarf	porch	world	err	mirth	hurt
swarm	sort	worm	merge	squirm	turn
quart	force	worth	serve	third	curve
quartz	gorge	worse	verse	whirl	urge

❈ Thoughts on Teaching the Vowel Sounds

Teachers and parents often ask about the order in which to teach the vowel sounds. My response (which some people don't find very satisfying) is: "In whatever order is best for the students." Guided by this principle, one should consider the students' ages (because some vowel sounds occur mostly in words that are not particularly useful to young children) and the skills they have already mastered or can learn quickly. A crucial skill for efficient decoding is blending, which is discussed in Chapter V. If a student already is good at blending, or quickly learns to blend efficiently, then the consonant and vowel sounds should be taught as fast as the student can learn them and can read words containing them. If a student has difficulty learning to blend accurately and efficiently, much work on words containing a limited number of different sounds seems to be best.

With all students, I teach all three sounds (long, short, and schwa) for a single vowel at the same time. I generally start with *a* because so many commonly used words can be made with single consonants and the *a* in closed and magic-e syllables (e.g., *can, pat, rag, sad, same, take, cane*); then, with the addition of a few sight words (e.g., *the, to, is*), short sentences can be practiced. In fact, there are about a hundred c v c words with *a* as the vowel, including names, and the meanings for fifty or sixty of them (excluding the names) would be known by most first graders. There are about ninety single-syllable, magic-e words with single consonants and *a*, and about forty-five to fifty-five of them would be understood by most first graders. This provides lots of practice, even for students who are quite slow to learn the blending process and/or the sounds for the consonants. I generally teach the three sounds for *i* next, moving to it even before the students have learned all the consonants if they are mastering the blending process well. I always try to contrast closed and magic-e syllables right from the beginning and move to a second vowel as quickly as possible, for two major reasons. First, it forces the student to pay attention to the particular letters *and* to the syllable structure (which determines the vowel sound) at the beginning of the reading process, thus establishing right away two of the most important processes for decoding. Second, it is more difficult for beginning readers to process words that are visually similar than words that differ; closed and magic-e words vary in length and in the appearance of the vowel grapheme (*a* vs. *a_e*).

When closed and magic-e syllables with *a* and *i* are mastered, decisions about what to teach next are based on how useful the words are and how efficient the blending process has become. If the students can blend well enough to decode some unfamiliar words or some pseudowords (non-real-word syllables such as *cag* and *jal*) with almost no hesitancy between the separate sounds of the syllable, then they will be able to transfer what they have already learned about the *a* and *i* sounds in closed and magic-e syllables to the rest of the vowels without needing much practice beyond the words they are reading. Therefore, I teach the long, short, and schwa sounds for *e, o,* and *u*, then spend about thirty seconds each day for a week or so having the students practice giving the sounds of the vowels in closed and magic-e syllables; however, I do not spend time having them read words out of context. Just learning the vowel sounds and practicing those sounds in words will give the students the skills they need to read these words in their stories.

Generally, I teach the sounds for the *a*-vowel teams next, using the skate as a mnemonic device. For very young children, I often teach only the teams *ai, ay, aw, wa, all, alt,* and *alk.* These are the ones that occur commonly in reading that is appropriate for first and second graders. Sometimes I add *augh* when the others are mastered; many children like to have long, challenging words to work on, and the *augh* words are very easy once they see *augh* as a single grapheme. (Thus, *c augh t* has the same number of phonemes as *cat,* which becomes apparent if you write *c ô t* above *caught*). For older students, I teach the entire skate and have them practice reading words containing each of the vowel teams.

At some point, the students need to begin learning the patterns for adding suffixes to monosyllables. I like to wait until they are becoming quite automatic at blending because an extra phoneme or syllable is being added to the words, which increases the difficulty of the blending process. Also, I want them to think of each word as a meaningful unit for which the meaning is being altered in a very precise and predictable way; if the students are still struggling with the blending process, they usually can't read the words with the added suffixes fluently enough to respond automatically with the meanings. Sometimes I start teaching the suffix patterns before beginning the *a*-vowel teams, and sometimes I start after the skate has been memorized while the students are beginning to read *a*-vowel team words. At this point, the students can also start reading compound words made up of the words that they can already decode (e.g., *sandman, backpack*).

After the *a*-vowel teams, I usually teach the vowel-r-closed syllables, using the star to teach the graphemes and phonemes. These syllables are extremely common in reading materials for all age levels, and they are easy to teach because they have only one sound for each vowel-r unit. I then look at the differences between vowel-r-magic-e syllables and magic-e syllables, specifically comparing the sounds of *-are* with the *-ace* graphemes and *-ire* with the *-ice* graphemes in words (*care* and *came, tire* and *time,* and so forth). These words are mastered very quickly, even by students who have not already transferred what they learned about magic-e syllables to words with *r* as the ending consonant. The vowel-r-vowel-team sounds are generally similar to the vowel-team sounds in the same way that the *-are* and *-ace* graphemes are similar (*aim* and *air, deep* and *deer, clean* and *clear, road* and *roar*), though some of them do not match (e.g., the sound of *ea* in *earn* and *earth* has no *e*-vowel team counterpart). There are not many monosyllabic words containing VR-VTs, so I wait until a VR-VT starts appearing in reading material before contrasting it with the appropriate vowel team.

The order in which the rest of the vowel-teams are taught is not at all crucial, and I often let my students decide which picture to explore next. In a classroom where the pictures are up on the walls, many students who have good memory abilities and are good at transferring learning strategies to new material will learn the rest of the vowel-teams as they are reading books. The students who have reading disabilities usually will need direct instruction and practice, but this is easy and moves quite quickly because they know the procedures they will be using to learn the new material.

I teach the open syllable structure while working on the vowel-r patterns. With third-grade or older students, I then often introduce the -_cle_ words while beginning the third vowel-team picture; this teaches them a syllable-division pattern and the rhythm of decoding two-syllable words. I then move to the VCCV syllable division pattern, using closed, open, vowel-r, and magic-e syllables, and continue to teach the vowel-team pictures and words as the students learn to read two-syllable words. The VCV syllable division pattern comes next, after which the students are ready to begin working on the rest of the multisyllable word skills, including the rest of the suffixes and the prefixes. Although this sequence is somewhat more confusing for a teacher to keep track of, the students are able to read trade books much more easily and accurately than if all the single-syllable word skills are completed before teaching the syllable division rules. At this stage, even the more disabled readers know enough about word structure and decoding strategies to be able to decode many words they have not been taught explicitly. By this time, also, they can read enough words fluently so that it is not terribly inefficient to rely on context to help them decode a few words now and then.[2]

For the most part, then, the order in which the vowel sounds and syllable structures are taught is not particularly important. While blending skills are developing, the words encountered should have fairly simple sounds and be commonly used by the learner. With older readers who are poor or disabled, moving quickly to two-syllable words enhances their self-esteem and motivates them to stick with the learning task even when it is difficult. It is also important with these older students to assess what they already know, so that they are not asked to relearn words they can already read.

---

[2]The research shows that good readers do not often rely on context to figure out words because they decode very fast and accurately, and that it is only the poor readers who frequently rely on context because they can't decode well enough to read the words as they come to them.

Many programs for teaching phonics are available, and they use a variety of sequences for introducing the sounds and spelling patterns. Very little research has compared the effectiveness and efficiency of these programs. However, two small studies in the 1970s demonstrated that teaching the syllable structures as concepts significantly improved the speed with which children learned to decode a variety of words and taught the children skills that they could use to read words with new sounds that they had not practiced during the teaching sessions.

I have consistently stressed the importance of the efficiency with which a sequence or activity teaches a decoding skill. This is particularly relevant when teaching decoding because decoding is only one part—albeit a crucial part—of the reading task. Since written English is an alphabetic language, readers must learn to decode in order to read an author's words, but this is just a means to an end. The goal of reading is to understand what the author is saying. Thus, decoding should be mastered as quickly and easily as possible, so that more time can be spent on developing the skills needed for understanding and appreciating the meaning of authors' words.

Appendix B

Prefixes and Suffixes

△▽△▽△▽△▽△▽△▽△▽△▽△▽△▽△▽△▽△▽△▽△▽△▽△▽△▽△▽△

These are alphabetical lists of affixes that habitual readers might encounter relatively often. Mindful of the richness, diversity, and flexibility of English, I make no claim for the completeness of this listing. Some affixes do not appear here because their meanings are confined largely to technical contexts, some because they are more appropriately considered as combining forms used to make compound words, and some because of my subjective judgment as to their usefulness in this book. In particular, the affixes that are used almost exclusively in science or medicine are not included, even though some of them are widely known because of one or two commonly used words (e.g., *carcinoma, methanol*). Moreover, the meanings given here are not exhaustive. In some cases, a single prefix or suffix many have half a dozen or more meanings, some very different from others, and the less common ones have been omitted.

⟨⟨⟨⟩ Prefixes ⟨⟨⟨⟩

a- (**an-** before vowels) in, on, at, to, up, out of, not, without, of, off [*aboard, anesthetic, asymmetric*]

ab- (**a-** before *m*, *p*, or *v*; **abs-** before *c* or *t*) away from, down from [*abstain, abdicate*]

ad- (also **ac-** before *c* or *q*, **af-** before *f*, **ag-** before *g*, **al-** before *l*, **an-** before *n*, **ap-** before *p*, **ar-** before *r*, **as-** before *s*, **at-** before *t*) to, toward; at; added to; near [*advance, adjoin, append*]

alti- (also **alto-**) high [*altitude, altimeter*]

ambi- both [*ambidextrous, ambivalent*]

amphi- on both sides; around [*amphibious, amphitheater*]

ana- upward; backward; again [*anachronism, Anabaptist*]

ante- in front of, before [*anteroom, antebellum*]

anti- (**ant-** before vowels) against, opposed to, counteractive [*antidote, antipathy*]

apo- (also **ap-**, **aph-** before vowels) away from; separated from, lacking [*apogee, aphesis*]

arch- chief, principal [*archangel, archdeacon*]

auto- (**aut-** before vowels) of, for, or by oneself or itself [*autobiography, automobile, autonomy*]

be- a wide range of meanings, including: around; thoroughly; away; cause to exist; cover with; furnish with; treat as [*beset, befriend, becalm*]

bene- good, well [*benediction, beneficial*]

bi- (also **bin-** before vowels, **bis-** before *c* or *s*) two, double [*bipartisan, biweekly, binoculars*]

bio- of living things [*biography, biodegradable*]

by- close, near; aside from; secondary to [*bystander, bypass, bylaw*]

cata- down; away; against [*cataclysm, catapult*]

centi- (also **cent-**) hundred; hundredth [*centipede, centimeter*]

circum- around, surrounding [*circumstance, circumference, circumlocution*]

cis- on the near side of [*cislunar, cisalpine*]

co- (a common variant of **com-**) jointly, mutually, together with; complement of [*coworker, cosine*]

com- (also **col-** before *l*; **con-** before *c, d, g, j, n, q, s, t,* and *v*; **cor-** before *r*; **co-** before *h, w,* and all vowels) with, together [*compound, companion, collect, concur, corroborate, cooperate*]

contra- against, opposed to [*contradict, contraband*]

de- away from; down from; the reverse [*depart, decline, decompose*]

deca- (also **dec-** before vowels) ten [*decagon, decameter, decade*]

deci- one tenth [*decibel, decimeter*]

demi- half; smaller, less [*demigod, demitasse*]

di- two, twice, double [*dihedral, dioxide, dipole*]

dia- (also **di-**) through; across; apart; between [*diagonal, diagram, dialect*]

dis- (also **di-** before *b, d, g, l, m, n, r, v;* **dif-** before *f*) opposite, lack of, removal or rejection of [*disobedient, disarray, disorderly, discontinue, disbar*]

dodeca- (also **dodec-** before vowels) twelve [*dodecagon, dodecaphonic*]

duo- (also **du-**) two [*duologue, duplex*]

dys- abnormal, difficult, impaired [*dysfunctional, dyslexia*]

en- (also **em-** before *p, b, m*) put into or on, get into or on; be within; cover with; become like; provide with [*encase, enact, endanger, empower*]

epi- (also **ep-** before vowels, **eph-** in aspirated words) on, upon; around; over; next to; besides; among; after [*epicenter, epigraph, epilogue*]

equi- equal [*equilateral, equinox*]

eu- good, well, beneficial [*eulogy, euphemism, euthanasia*]

ex- (also **e-** before *b, d, g, l, m, n, r, v,* **ec-** before *c* or *s,* **ef-** before *f,* **es-** in many words of French origin) out of, away from; beyond; thoroughly; upward; without [*exclude, exhale, extricate, evolve, effluent*]

extra- outside the scope of, beyond [*extraordinary, extrasensory, extraterrestrial*]

for- away, off; very much, completely, intensely [*forswear, forbid, forfend*]

fore- preceding in time, place, or order; at the front of [*foremost, forerunner, foredeck*]

giga- billion [*gigabyte, gigahertz*]

hecto- (also **hect-** before vowels) hundred [*hectoliter, hectometer*]

hemi- half [*hemisphere, hemicycle*]

hepta- (also **hept-** before vowels) seven [*heptagon, heptarchy*]

hetero- (**heter-** before vowels) other, different [*heterodox, heterosexual*]

hexa- (also **hex-** before vowels) six [*hexagon, hexagram, hexameter*]

homeo- (also **homoeo-, homoio-**) like, similar [*homeopathic, homeomorphism*]

homo- (also **hom-** before vowels) same, like [*homogeneous, homonym*]

hyper- over, above; abnormally more than, excessive [*hyperactive, hypersensitive*]

hypo- (also **hyp-** before vowels) underneath, below; abnormally less than; incomplete [*hypodermic, hypoglycemia*]

in- (also **il-** before *l;* **im-** before *m, p,* and *b;* **ir-** before *r*) in, into, within, on; toward; not, lacking; make happen [*inbreed, incline, illiterate, imperil*]

inter- between or among; together, mutual [*interchange, interrupt, intersect*]

intro- in, into, inward, within [*introduce, introspective*]

iso- (also **is-** before vowels) equal, similar, identical [*isometric, isotope, isosceles*]

kilo- thousand [*kilogram, kilometer, kilowatt*]

macro- large, long [*macrobiotic, macroeconomics, macroscopic*]

magni- large, great [*magnification, magniloquence*]

mal- bad(ly), wrong(ly) [*maladjusted, malpractice, maltreat*]

mega- million; large, great [*megabyte, megalith, megaphone*]

megalo- large or great, perhaps abnormally or strikingly so [*megalomania, magalopolis*]

meta- (also **met-** before vowels) beyond, transcending, higher; changing, changed; later, behind, at the back of [*metaphysical, metaphor, metamorphosis*]

micro- (also **micr-**) small; extremely small [*microbiology, microfilm, micrometer, microscopic*]

mid- in or at the middle of [*midair, midday, midshipman*]

milli- one thousandth [*milligram, millimeter*]

mini- smaller or lesser than [*miniskirt, minivan*]

mis- wrong, bad, unsuitable, in error [*misbehave, mistake, mismanage*]

mono- one, single, alone [*monotone, monograph*]

multi- (also **mult-** before vowels) many, much; more than two [*multicolored, multilateral*]

nano- one billionth; extremely small [*nanosecond, nanometer, nanoplankton*]

neo- new, recent [*neoclassic, neocolonial, neolithic*]

non- not [*nonviolent, nonsense*]

nona- nine [*nonagenarian, nonagon*]

ob- (also **o-** before *m*, **oc-** before *c*, **of-** before *f*, **op-** before *p*) to, toward; in front of; against; up over; completely; inversely [*obscure, object, omit, oppose*]

octa- (also **oct-**, **octo-**) eight, eighth [*octagon, octennial, octogenarian*]

oligo- (also **olig-** before vowels) small, few [*oligopoly, oligarchy*]

omni- all, all-inclusive [*omnipotent, omniscient, omnivorous*]

ortho- correct, proper, standard [*orthodontist, orthodox*]

pan- encompassing, applying, or common to all [*panacea, Pan-American, pandemic*]

para- (also **par-**) beside, alongside, beyond, to one side, aside from, subsidiary to [*paraphrase, paraprofessional, paramilitary*]

penta- (also **pent-** before vowels) five [*pentagon, pentagram, Pentateuch, pentathlon*]

per- through, throughout; thoroughly, completely; away [*perceive, perforate, persist*]

peri- around, about; surrounding, enclosing; near [*periscope, perimeter, perigee*]

pico- one trillionth [*picometer, picosecond*]

poly- many, much, more than one; abnormally or unusually many [*polyandry, polychrome, polygot, polynomial*]

post- after in time, later than; after in position, behind [*postpone, postscript*]

pre- (also **prae-**) before in time, earlier than; before in position, in front of; before in rank; preliminary to [*preheat, predestination, precedent, preschool*]

pro- supporting, defending; substituting for, acting for; before in place or time; forward or ahead of [*proponent, pronoun, progress*]

proto- (also **prot-** before vowels) earliest, first, original [*protocol, protoplasm, prototype*]

pseudo- (also **pseud-** before vowels) false, dishonest, unreal; deceptively like [*pseudonym, pseudoscience*]

psycho- pertaining to the mind or to mental processes [*psychodrama, psychology, psychotherapy*]

quadri- (also **quadra-**, **quadru-**, **quadr-**) four [*quadrilateral, quadraphonic, quadruped, quadrennial*]

quint- five, fifth [*quintessence, quintillion, quintuplet*]

re- back, backwards; again, anew [*return, reconstruct*]

semi- half; partially [*semiannual, semicircle, semiautomatic*]

septi- (also **sept-** before vowels) seven, seventh [*septilateral, septuagenarian*]

sex- six [*sexagesimal, sexennial, sextuplet*]

sub- (also **suc-** before *c*, **suf-** before *f*, **sug-** before *g*, **sum-** before *m*, **sup-** before *p*, **sur-** before *r*, **sus-** before *c*, *p*, and *t*) under, below, beneath; lower in rank or position [*submarine, subculture, subordinate, support, suspend*]

super- above, over, beyond; higher in rank or position; better or more than usual [*supernatural, superficial, superintendent, supersede*]

sur- over, above, beyond [*surcharge, surrealism*]

syn- (also **syl-** before *l*; **sym-** before *b*, *m*, and *p*; **sys-** before *s* and aspirate *h*) together with, at the same time [*synchronize, symphony*]

tele- (also **tel-**) from or across a distance [*telegraph, telepathy, telephone, television*]

tera- one trillion [*terahertz, teraohm*]

tetra- (also **tetr-** before vowels) four [*tetrahedron, tetrarch, tetroxide*]

trans- (also **tra-** before *d*, *j*, *l*, *m*, *n*, and *v*) across, over; through; above and beyond; to change [*transport, transcript, transform, traduce*]

tri- three, third, triple [*triangle, trident, tripod*]

ultra- beyond, out of range of; excessive, extreme [*ultrasonic, ultraviolet, ultramodern*]

un- not; lack of; opposite or contrary to; reverse or removal [*unpleasant, untested, unwind*]

under- beneath, below; referring to a lower position; less than the normal or standard degree or amount of [*undercarriage, undersecretary, underachiever*]

uni- one, single [*unicycle, unicorn, uniform*]

vice- a person substituting for, acting in place of; deputy [*viceroy, vicegerent*]

with- away, back, against [*withdraw, withhold, withstand*]

❬❭ Suffixes ❬❭

-ability (noun-forming, corr. to *-able*) [*transferability, marketability*]

-able (adj.-forming; also **-ible**; **-ably** and **-ibly** for forming adverbs) able to, capable of; worthy of; inclined or susceptible to; having the quality or qualities of [*transferable, presentable, fallible, trainable*]

-acious (adj.-forming) tending towards, having a lot of [*fallacious, voracious*]

-acity (noun-forming, corr. to **-acious**) [*tenacity, perspicacity*]

-ad to, toward; related to [*triad, olympiad*]

-ade (noun-forming) the act, result, or product of; a sweetened drink made of [*blockade, lemonade*]

-age (noun-forming) condition, act, or effect of; location of; connection with; cost of [*marriage, orphanage, appendage, postage*]

-al (adj.-forming) like, pertaining to, connected with [*comical, annual*] (noun-forming) act or process of [*trial*]

-algia (noun-forming) pain of [*neuralgia, nostalgia*]

-an (adj.- and noun-forming) belonging to, related to; a member or follower of [*diocesan, Californian, Mohammedan*]

-ana (noun-forming) material such as facts, anecdotes, pictures, writings of or about [*Americana*]

-ance (also **-ancy**) (noun-forming) the act, quality, or condition of; something used for [*inheritance, conveyance*]

-ant (adj.-forming, corr. to *-ance*) having, exhibiting, or doing something [*radiant, compliant*] (noun-forming) a person or thing that does or causes something [*occupant, deodorant*]

-ar (adj.-forming) like, relating to, characterized by [*singular, insular*] (noun-forming) person with a particular function [*scholar, bursar*]

-arch (noun-forming) ruler, leader [*matriarch, monarch*]

-archy (noun-forming) ruling; that which is ruled [*oligarchy, monarchy*]

-ard (noun-forming; also **-art**) one who is or does something to excess [*drunkard, braggart*]

-arian (adj.- and noun-forming) signifies age, religious or social belief, occupation [*nonagenarian, Unitarian, vegetarian, agrarian*]

-arium (noun-forming) a building, place, or structure for [*aquarium, solarium, terrarium*]

-ary (adj.- and noun-forming) related to, connected with, of, for [*auxiliary, elementary, missionary, functionary, bestiary*]

-ate (verb-forming) various meanings: make, become, form, produce, provide, etc. [*operate, rejuvenate*] (adj.-forming) having the features of, filled with [*sensate, affectionate*] (noun-forming) an office or official [*potentate, triumvirate*]

-atic (adj.-forming) having the property or characteristic of [*aromatic, chromatic, Hanseatic*]

-ation (noun-forming) process of; state or condition of; result of [*verification, civilization, dramatization*]

-ative (adj.-forming) relating to, having the nature of, tending to [*informative, provocative, ruminative*]

-ator (noun-forming) someone who or something that does [*refrigerator, procrastinator*]

-atory (adj.-forming) related to, characterized by, resulting from [*commendatory, exclamatory*]

-burg (also **-burgh**) city, town, village, etc. [*Lynchburg, Pittsburgh*]

-cade procession, parade [*cavalcade, motorcade*]

-chrome color, colored [*monochrome, mercurochrome*]

-cidal (adj.-forming, corr. to *-cide*) of a killer or killing; able to kill [*homicidal, herbicidal*]

-cide (noun-forming) killer or killing of [*genocide, insecticide*]

-cle small [*cubicle, icicle, particle*]

-cule small [*minuscule, molecule*]

-cy (noun-forming) quality, condition, state of being; position or rank of [*adequacy, confederacy, presidency*]

-dom (noun-forming) rank or position of; domain of; fact or condition of; all who are [*stardom, fiefdom, boredom, Christendom*]

-ean (adj.- and noun-forming) belonging or pertaining to, derived from [*crustacean, Euclidean, European*]

-ed (also **-t**) used to form past tense and past participle of most verbs [*learned, recited, camped, burnt*] (adj.-forming) having, provided with, characterized by [*feathered, striped*]

-ee (noun-forming) recipient of; someone in a specified condition [*grantee, payee, absentee*]

-eer (noun-forming) someone who does, makes, operates, or is somehow related to [*balladeer, puppeteer, racketeer*] (verb-forming) to do or be concerned with a specified thing [*commandeer, electioneer, volunteer*]

-en (verb-forming) cause a specified condition, come to have a specified characteristic [*loosen, ripen*] (adj.-forming) made up of, having, resembling [*earthen, oaken*] also used to form the past participles of some verbs [*given, taken*]

-ence (noun-forming; also **ency**) same as *-ance* [*sustinence, consistency*]

-enne female who does or has to do with [*comedienne, equestrienne*]

-ent (adj.- and noun-forming, corr. to *ence*) same as *-ant* [*consistent, fluorescent, agent*]

-eous (adj.-forming) having the nature or characteristic of [*courageous, homogeneous, miscellaneous*]

-er (noun-forming; also **-ier**; **-yer** after *w*) a person or thing that is or does a specified thing; someone who comes from a specified place [*teacher, New Yorker, glazier, sawyer*]   also makes the comparative form of adjectives and adverbs [*fuller, prettier*]

-ern tending toward a specified direction [*southern, western*]

-ery (noun-forming; also **-ry**) a place to or for; the practice or craft of; a collection of a certain kind; the behavior or attitude of [*cannery, artistry, jewelry, bravery*]

-es makes the plural form of some nouns; indicates the third person singular, present indicative form of some verbs [*witches, teaches*]

-escence (noun-forming, corr. to *-escent*) a beginning or ongoing state [*acquiescence, obsolescence*]

-escent (adj.-forming) starting to be something specified; exhibiting or reflecting [*adolescent, fluorescent*]

-ese (adj.- and noun-forming) a native or inhabitant of; the language, dialect, or style of [*Maltese, Brooklynese, legalese*]

-esque (adj.-forming) resembling, in the style or manner of [*statuesque, Romanesque*]

-ess female [*deaconess, waitress*]

-est the superlative degree of most one- or two-syllable adjectives and adverbs [*brightest, laziest, sweetest*]

-et little, small [*baronet, cygnet*]

-eth signifies ordinal form for some numerical words (see also *-th*); archaic ending of the third person singular, present indicative, of verbs [*twentieth, fiftieth, abideth, believeth*]

-etic (adj.-forming) related to, displaying the characteristics of [*apologetic, genetic, phonetic*]

-ette   small; female; an imitation of [*diskette, suffragette, leatherette*]

-fer (noun-forming) carrier or producer of [*conifer, lucifer*]

-ferous (adj.-forming, corr. to *-fer*) carrying, producing [*floriferous, vociferous*]

-fic (adj.-forming) making, creating, or causing [*honorific, specific*]

-fold having a specified number of parts; multiplied by a specified number or a specific number of times greater [*manifold, fourfold, hundredfold*]

-form having the form or shape of [*cruciform, cuneiform, dentiform*]

-fuge (noun-forming) something that expels or drives away from [*centrifuge, vermifuge*]

-ful (adj.- and noun-forming) filled with, having the characteristics of; able or inclined to; an amount that would fill [*colorful, helpful, spoonful*]

-fy (verb-forming) make, form, cause to become, have, or feel [*beautify, magnify, petrify, verify*] (This is one of the few cases in which a *y* at the end of a multisyllable word says /ī/, rather than /ē/.)

-genous (adj.-forming) producing, generating; produced by, coming from [*androgenous, erogenous, indigenous*]

-genic (adj.-forming) formed from or produced by; suited to [*cryogenic, hallucinogenic, photogenic*]

-graph (noun-forming) something that writes, draws, or records; something that is written, drawn, or recorded in some way (verb-forming) to write, draw, or record in some way [*telegraph, photograph*]

-hood (noun-forming) state or condition; the whole group of a specified kind [*adulthood, falsehood, sisterhood*]

-ia (noun-forming) used in forming names of countries, diseases, plants etc.; used to form some plural or collective nouns [*Lithuania, amnesia, lobelia, memorabilia*]

-ibility (noun-forming, corr. to *-ible*) [*credibility, fallibility*]

-ible Same as *-able* [*accessible, tangible*]

-ic (adj.- and noun-forming) of, pertaining to, like, having the characteristic of [*acrobatic, basic, cynic, historic, optic*]

-ical (adj.-forming) same as *-ic*, except that adjectives formed with this suffix sometimes have meanings distinct from the corresponding *-ic* forms [*astronomical, cynical, historical, optical, technical*]

-ician (noun-forming) a practitioner or specialist in [*beautician, mathematician, physician*]

-ics (noun-forming) the science, art, practices, or system of [*aerobics, dramatics, graphics, physics*]

-ile (adj.- and noun-forming; also **-il**) related to, capable of, suitable for [*fragile, percentile, civil*]

-ina used for the feminine form of names, titles, etc. [*ballerina, Katrina, tsarina*]

-ine pertaining to, resembling [*alkaline, equine, leonine, saline*]

-ing forms the present participle of verbs [*flying, going*] (noun-forming) the act or an instance of; a result of the action of; something that acts to; material used for [*airing, blessing, casing, paneling*]

-ion (noun-forming) act or result of; state of being [*coercion, impression, rebellion, tension*]

-ious (adj.-forming, sometimes corr. to *-ion*) characterized by, filled with [*furious, rebellious, religious*]

-ish (adj.-forming) of or belonging to; like, having the qualities of; tending to; somewhat [*English, childish, greenish, smallish*]

-ism (noun-forming) action, practice, or process of ; state of being; quality or behavior that is characteristic of; the doctrine, theory, or principle of; a distinctive example of [*criticism, autism, fanaticism, behaviorism, Protestantism, legalism*]

-ist (noun-forming, corr. to *-ism*) a person who does, makes, produces, etc.; a skilled practitioner of; an adherent or proponent of [*motorist, behaviorist, biologist, feminist*]

-istic (adj.-forming, corr. to *-ism* and *-ist*) [*behavioristic, capitalistic, legalistic*]

-ite (noun-forming) a native or inhabitant of; a partisan of; a particular type of chemical [*suburbanite, Darwinite, sulphite*]

-ition (noun-forming) same as *-ation* [*apparition, competition, opposition, superstition*]

-itious (adj.-forming, sometimes corr. to *-ition*) of, having the nature of, characterized by [*fictitious, superstitious*]

-itis (noun-forming) inflammatory disease or inflammation of [*laryngitis, meningitis*]

-itive (adj.-forming, sometimes corr. to *-ition*) same as *-ative* [*competitive, cognitive*]

-ity (noun-forming) state, quality, condition [*authenticity, curiosity, density, lucidity*]

-ive (adj.-forming) tending or inclined to, relating to [*disruptive, evasive, cursive, objective*]

-ize (verb-forming) cause to be or become; make or change into; make similar to; treat with; act in a specified way [*equalize, colonize, alphabetize, galvanize, philosophize*]

-kin small, little [*catkin, lambkin*]

-le various meanings, including: small; a thing used for; having a tendency toward; used to emphasize frequency [*jiggle, nibble, handle, brittle, sparkle*]

-lence (noun-forming, corr. to *-lent*) [*corpulence, fraudulence, virulence*]

-lent (adj.-forming) having a lot of, filled with, distinguished by [*corpulent, fraudulent, virulent*]

-less (adj.-forming) lack of, freedom from [*hopeless, motionless, boundless*]

-let little, small; a bandlike object worn on some part of the body [*piglet, wavelet, anklet, bracelet*]

-like (adj.-forming) resembling, typical of, appropriate for [*lifelike, catlike, statesmanlike*]

-ling (added to nouns) small; having a connection (often unimportant or disreputable) with [*duckling, fledgling, sapling, hireling, underling*]

-ly (adj.-forming) resembling, characteristic of, suitable to; happening once every specified period of time [*brotherly, elderly, ghostly, bimonthly, daily*] (adv.-forming) in a specified manner, to a specified extent, at a specified time interval, in a specified direction, order, place, etc. [*candidly, profoundly, annually, westerly*]

-man (noun-forming) a person (not necessarily male) who does, uses, or is characterized by [*chairman, cameraman, selectman*] (This is a separate word used so often in compounds that it is sometimes regarded as a suffix.)

-ment (noun-forming) result or product; means; act, action, or process; state, condition, or degree [*development, easement, accompaniment, puzzlement*]

-meter a device for measuring something [*altimeter, telemeter, thermometer*]

-metry the science or method of measuring [*audiometry, colorimetry, trigonometry, telemetry*]

-mony (noun-forming) something that is the result or condition of [*acrimony, matrimony, testimony*]

-most used to form superlatives, esp. of adjectives and adverbs denoting position or location [*southernmost, uppermost*]

-ness (noun-forming) state, quality, or condition of being [*aloofness, bullheadedness, crabbiness, loudness*]

-ode way, path; resembling [*cathode, diode, nematode*]

-oid (adj.- and noun-forming) like, similar to [*asteroid, cycloid, mongoloid, ovoid*]

-ology (noun-forming) the study of or body of knowledge about [*audiology, psychology, toxicology*]

-or (noun-forming) person or thing that is or does a specified thing; quality or condition (often **-our** in British usage) [*actor, surveyor, honor, honour*]

-orium (noun-forming) a building or place for [*auditorium, sanitorium*]

-ory (adj.-forming) having the nature of or a tendency toward [*auditory, illusory, sensory*] (noun-forming) a place or thing for [*directory, observatory*]

-ose (adj.-forming) having the characteristics of, filled with [*comatose, verbose*]

-osis state, condition, or process; an abnormal or diseased condition [*mitosis, osmosis, symbiosis, neurosis, psychosis, silicosis*]

-osity (noun-forming, corr. to some *-ose* or *-ous* adjectives) [*curiosity, monstrosity, pomposity, verbosity*]

-otic (adj.-forming, corr. to *-osis*) affected by or with; causing, producing [*symbiotic, neurotic, psychotic*]

-ous (adj.-forming) having, full of [*curious, mischievous, monstrous, pompous*]

-phile (noun-forming) a person who likes or loves a specified thing [*audiophile, bibliophile, Francophile, zoophile*]

-phobe (noun-forming) a person who fears or hates a specified thing [*claustrophobe, Francophobe, xenophobe*]

-phony (noun-forming) sound of a specified kind [*cacophony, symphony*]

-ship (noun-forming) the quality or condition of; the status, rank or profession of; the art or function of; the collectivity of all individuals of a specified class [*friendship, lordship, musicianship, readership*]

-sion (noun-forming) the act, process, or result of [*collision, division, inversion*]

-some (adj.-forming) having or producing the quality of, tending to [*awesome, irksome, troublesome*] (noun-forming, used with numeral words) a specified number, usually of people [*twosome, threesome, foursome*]

-ster (noun-forming) a person who creates, does, or is something specified; a person associated with [*pollster, songster, teamster, mobster*]

-stress (feminine form corr. to *-ster*) [*seamstress, songstress*]

-teen ten and (used for cardinal numbers 13 through 19) [*thirteen, fourteen, nineteen*]

-th (noun-forming; also **-t**) the act or result of; the state or quality of [*growth, health, length*] (adj.-forming; also **-eth** after vowels) used for ordinal numerals [*fourth, seventh, twentieth*]

-tion (noun-forming) the act, process, state, or result of [*injection, digestion, contribution, infection*]

-tious (adj.-forming, sometimes corr. to *-tion*) having the property of, the result of [*ambitious, infectious, malicious, surreptitious*]

-trix (noun-forming; feminine form corr. to *-or*) [*aviatrix, benefactrix*]

-tude (noun-forming) condition, state, or instance of being [*aptitude, gratitude, quietude, solitude*]

-ty (noun-forming) quality or condition of; times ten [*activity, certainty, morality, eighty*]

-ular (adj.-forming) related to, resembling [*molecular, triangular*]

-ule (noun-forming) small [*ductule, globule*]

-ulent (adj.-forming) filled with, having an abundance of, characterized by [*corpulent, turbulent, virulent*]

-ulous (adj.-forming) having a tendency toward, full of, characterized by [*querulous, ridiculous, scrupulous*]

-ure (noun-forming) act, process, result, or state of being; a function or an agent or body that performs a function [*architecture, composure, creature, erasure, procedure, legislature*]

-ward (also **-wards**) in a specified direction or toward a specified objective [*backward, backwards, homeward, westward*]

-ways (adv.-forming) in a specified manner, direction, or position [*crossways, edgeways, sideways*]

-wise (adv.-forming) in a specified manner, direction, or position; in a way characteristic of; with regard to [*crosswise, lengthwise, clockwise, otherwise, weatherwise*]

-wright (noun-forming) a person who makes or fixes [*playwright, wheelwright*] (Like *-man*, this is actually a separate word used so often in compounds that it is sometimes regarded as a suffix.)

-y (also **-ey**, **-ie**) little, dear (used in forming diminutives and nicknames) [*Billy, Billie, cutie, horsey*] (adj.-forming) having, characterized by, resembling, tending to, suggestive of [*curly, gooey, messy, rainy, horsy*] (noun-forming) state or quality of being; goods of a specified kind, or a place where they are made or sold; a collective body of a specified kind; action or activity [*jealousy, millinery, academy, blasphemy*]

△▽△▽△▽△▽△▽△▽△▽△▽△▽△▽△▽△

Answers

for

Exercise Sheets

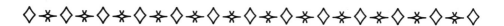

SORTING SINGLE-SOUND CONSONANT TEAMS AND BLENDS

bl a ck squ id la mb wh i zz spl i nt sm e lt gr a ph

gn a sh wr i st fr i sk kn ave th i nk spr u ng

thr ice pn euma cl u tch shr ike str oke scr u nch

sw i ft cr y pt ch i mp ps alm tr i ll pl e dge qu it

SSCTs		BLENDS	
ck	pn	bl	cl
mb	tch	squ	shr
wh	ch	spl	str
zz	ps	nt	scr
ph	ll	sm	nch
gn	dge	lt	sw
sh	qu**	gr	ft
wr		st	cr
kn		fr	pt
th		sk	mp
nk*		spr	tr
ng*		thr	pl

*   Remember that *nk* and *ng* are SSCTs because their sounds are not the
sound of *n, k,* and *g* by themselves or in blends such as *nd.*

** If you categorized the *qu* under blends, you are technically correct.
Review the note accompanying *qu* in Appendix A, Sounds for
Consonants and Consonant Teams, page 99, for why it is called a SSCT.

SORTING MAGIC-E AND OTHER MARKER-E SYLLABLES

rake   dance   please   Steve   ice   fudge   spume
graze   sconce   niece   cringe   slide   prune
shame   dunce   mauve   rose   flounce   quote
scribe   cruise   fence   ode   ease   change   flute

MAGIC-E	OTHER MARKER-E
rake	dance
Steve	please
ice	fudge
spume	sconce
graze	niece
slide	cringe
prune	dunce
shame	mauve
rose	flounce
quote*	cruise
scribe	fence
ode	ease
flute	change

* The *qu* is a consonant team, so the *ote* is a magic-e unit.

The vowel unit in every magic-e word should be <u>vce</u>. Any <u>vvce</u>, <u>vcce</u>, or <u>vvcce</u> should be under the "other marker-e" column.

SORTING CLOSED, MAGIC-E, AND VOWEL-TEAM SYLLABLES

chrome toll Gwen sloe phlox lash use pie
these choice sigh lace free log imp lawn
next flute stun ode fray up chew spice
gift quake think old true pine rude oz
aught peace phlegm ate stand time tone

CLOSED	MAGIC-E	VOWEL-TEAM
Gwen	chrome	toll
phlox	use	sloe
lash	these	pie
log	lace	choice **
imp	flute	sigh
next	ode	free
stun	spice	lawn
up	quake *	fray
gift	pine	chew
think	rude	old
oz	ate	true
phlegm	time	aught
stand	tone	peace **

* The qu is a consonant team, so the *ake* is a magic-e unit.

** The *e* at the end is a marker-e, marking the *c* (keeping it soft).

SORTING VOWEL-R-CLOSED AND CLOSED SYLLABLES

car   trump   hurl   sham   herd   work   left   firm
shunt   perk   dwarf   stint   horse   chop   charm
chant   best   warp   rich   short   stretch   pant
bird   stump   nurse   flock

VOWEL-R-CLOSED	**CLOSED**
car	trump
hurl	sham
herd	left
work	shunt
firm	stint
perk	chop
dwarf	chant
horse	best
charm	rich
warp	stretch
short	pant
bird	stump
nurse	flock

Remember that a marker-e does not control the sound of the v̲r̲ unit, so the words with a marker-e are categorized as vowel-r-closed syllables.

SORTING VOWEL-R-CLOSED, VOWEL-R-MAGIC-E, AND VOWEL-R-VOWEL-TEAM SYLLABLES

cart   dire   air   Thor   hear   tier   care   germ
Moore   lyre   clear   coarse   wore   fare   stir
flair   warm   shire   quart   terse   fierce   score
urge   hour   sphere   birch   pure   word   queer
here   square   rear   horde

VR-CLOSED	VR-MAGIC-E	VR-VOWEL-TEAM
cart	dire	air
Thor	care	hear
germ	lyre	tier
stir	wore	Moore
warm	fare	clear
quart *	shire	coarse
terse	score	flair
urge	sphere	fierce
birch	pure	hour
word	here	queer *
horde	square*	rear

*   The *qu* is a consonant unit that says /kw/. In *quart*, the *uar* has the sound of /war/. Note that the /w/ does not change the sound of the -*are* or the *eer* (*square*, *queer*).

USING THE DOUBLING RULE TO ADD SUFFIXES

The reasons for not doubling the consonant are marked above the words.

can + ing

canning

fish + es
  cc

fishes

step + ed

stepped

tax + ing
ks

taxing

jump + y
cc

jumpy

nut + y

nutty

tax + able
ks

taxable

dim + est

dimmest

sad + ly
   c

sadly

war + s
   c

wars

storm + y
   cc

stormy

harm + less
cc + c

harmless

star + y

starry

tar + ed

tarred

firm + ly
cc + c

firmly

stir + able

stirrable

spur + ed

spurred

market + ing

marketing

control + ed

controlled

forget + able

forgettable

sudden + ly

suddenly

transmit + ed

transmitted

allot + ment
    c

allotment

complex + ity
    ks

complexity

master + ing

mastering

admit + ance

admittance

pilot + ed

piloted

USING THE SILENT E RULE TO ADD SUFFIXES

The reasons for not dropping the *e* appear above the words or in the notes at the bottom of the page.

bike + s̥^c
bikes

square + er
squarer

dribble + ing
dribbling

cute + est
cutest

large + l̥y^c
largely

village + s̥^c
villages

scheme + ed
schemed

ice + y
icy

compete + ing
competing

time + l̥y^c
timely

crackle + y
crackly

capsize + ed
capsized

care + f̥ul^c
careful

singe + ing
_singeing_*

festive + ity
festivity

skate + ing
skating

serve + er
server

purple + ish
purplish

size + able
sizable

insane + l̥y^c
insanely

handle + ed
handled

dance + ing
dancing

accuse + atory
accusatory

excite + m̥ent^c
excitement

pure + est
purest

active + ate
activate

change + able
changeable**

*   Without the *e*, *singeing* becomes *singing*, a different word.
**   Without the *e*, *g* becomes /g/ before *a*.

ADDING SUFFIXES TO WORDS ENDING IN *Y*

The reasons for not changing the *y* to *i* are marked above the words.

try + ed
tried

lazy + er
lazier

yy
coy + ly
coyly

pry + es
pried

lazy + ly
lazily

spy + es
spies

y + i
pry + ing
prying

yy
gray + er
grayer

y + i
comply + ing
complying

monosyllable + ly
dry + ly
dryly

y + i
pacify + ing
pacifying

heavy + est
heaviest

yy
play + ful
playful

lazy + ness
laziness

family + ar
familiar

envy + able
enviable

lucky + ly
luckily

factory + es
factories

silly + est
silliest

weary + er
wearier

fury + ous
furious

y + i
decry + ing
decrying

y + i
sleepy + ish
sleepyish

marry + age
marriage

angry + est
angriest

library + an
librarian

yy
defray + ed
defrayed

Suggestions for Further Reading

⊗ The Acquisition of Reading Skills

- Adams, Marilyn (1990). *Beginning to read: Thinking and learning about print.* Cambridge, MA: The MIT Press.

    or

    Adams, Marilyn (1990). *Beginning to read: Thinking and learning about print. A summary.* Prepared by Steven A. Stahl, Jean Osborn, and Fran Lehr. Urbana-Champaign, IL: The Center for the Study of Reading.

    The complete book is very readable, even if you do not have an academic background in the psychology or teaching of reading. However, it does include discussions of much of the research that substantiates the ideas presented. The summary indicates what the research tends to show, but does not describe the research itself. It, too, is extremely readable, but because it summarizes a much larger book, each paragraph is tightly packed with important information.

- Chall, Jeanne S. (1983). *Stages of reading development.* New York: McGraw-Hill Book Company.

    Chall discusses the development of reading skills from pre-reading to proficient adult reading. She summarizes much of the research that has led to our knowledge about the acquisition of reading skills, in a manner that makes the ideas accessible even if you have no academic background in education or reading.

⊗ Phonemic Awareness

- Brady, Susan A., and Shankweiler, Donald P., eds. (1991). *Phonological processes in literacy. A tribute to Isabelle Y. Liberman.* Hillsdale, NJ: Lawrence Erlbaum Associates, Publishers.

    This book reports and discusses some of the most important research relating to the fields of language phonology and reading. Although very well

137

written, it contains quite a large body of vocabulary that is likely to be unfamiliar to those who do not have some background in reading or dyslexia. If, after reading Adams or Chall (above), you are interested in fine-tuning your understanding of how phonology and reading interact, you should find this book readable (though difficult) and extremely informative.

- Rosner, Jerome (1979). *Helping children overcome learning difficulties. A step-by-step guide for parents and teachers.* (2nd ed.) New York: Walker and Company.

    Rosner suggests many, many activities for use with pre-schoolers and with school-aged children. Although Rosner focused on children who have learning difficulties, the activities he describes are excellent for all children. Since the time Rosner wrote this book, a great deal has been learned about the difficulty levels of many activities he suggests. Knowing the more current research is not crucial for using these activities, however; just try a variety of them to find which ones provide success and enjoyment for the learner, and gradually add others.

    Rosner emphasized perceptual skills in addition to analysis skills. We now know that the auditory analysis skills are crucial for reading-decoding, but we do not yet know exactly which other perceptual and analysis skills are related to other aspects of the school curriculum. Thus, while development of these perceptual and analysis skills should not *replace* instruction in basic skills, they are important in and of themselves, and they may relate to ease of learning in school. As a reference for activities that parents and children can do together, this book is excellent.

- Stanovich, Keith E., ed. (1988). *Children's reading and the development of phonological awareness.* Detroit: Wayne State University Press.

    Stanovich is one of the most active researchers in the field of beginning reading skills. If you are interested in becoming current in this field, you should look for his writings and those of the people to whom he refers.

Index

4